SOMETHING'S HAPPENING HERE

A Memoir of the 60s

Dennis Hicks

Marco Press
Venice, CA 90291
drhicks2@yahoo.com
http://www.dennishicks.net

Copyright © 2017 by Dennis Hicks
All Rights Reserved

Printed in the United States of America
First Edition 2017

Cover design by Susan Dworski
susan@theblueone.com
Cover art: detail of painting
"The Playroom" 1967
by Dennis Hicks

ISBN: 0970909268
Library of Congress Control Number: 2017912795
ISBN: 9780970909268

To Stef
For your patience, support and insights
And for believing that I would come to trust our love

INTRODUCTION

This memoir covers the years 1964–1971. The reliability of my (or anyone's) memory of that period has been challenged by the quip, "If someone tells you about the 60s, they weren't there." The joke has to do with the mind-blowing effect of psychedelic drugs. But the greater truth is that the 60s were a particularly complex and chaotic period of American history. My effort to tell it like it was has been affected by memory, my subjective point of view, and my desire to tell a good story. In short, this memoir shares much with fiction: a few characters are composites; the conversations are approximations; and sometimes my old friends say and do things that they didn't actually say or do. Nonetheless, this remembrance accurately reflects my experience of the events and the spirit of that period. It is my hope that if you were there you'll recognize a great deal of it. If you weren't, you'll get a feeling of what made it so remarkable.

1

THE ORIGINS OF A RADICAL

The United States government wanted my ass. I had lost my student draft deferment when I graduated from college in June of 1964 and headed for New York to study painting. I wasn't too concerned, because the U.S. didn't need many guys beyond those who had volunteered. After all, there wasn't a real war going on, just some "policing actions" halfway around the world. No one, including my parents, suggested I was taking a big risk. Everything changed on the evening of August 4. President Johnson, who'd taken over after John Kennedy was assassinated the previous November, interrupted all three channels of national television to announce an "unprovoked" torpedo attack by a North Vietnamese ship on an American destroyer in the Gulf of Tonkin. He'd begun retaliatory bombing and asked Congress for the authority to conduct military operations in Southeast Asia. He got it without the benefit of a declaration of war, and America began grabbing up young men to turn into soldiers. It took them a while, but my California draft board finally got my forwarding address in New York City and demanded I show up at the Whitehall Street Induction Station in lower Manhattan on March 19, 1965.

I was taking classes at the renowned Art Students League, drawing nudes in the morning, painting all afternoon. I was an artist—or, at least, I wanted to be. I'd barely heard of Vietnam, North or South, and I had no idea why it was important. And I had no particular inclination to be a soldier: A hero, sure, but a soldier? When I thought about the draft, which was rarely, I was convinced I'd fail this "initial physical" because I had something wrong with a vertebra in my back. It had never really bothered me, but I had an X-ray to prove it. To be honest, I was a little disappointed. Like every boy I knew, I'd grown up playing war, turning into a soldier, a cowboy, or an Indian, depending on the need of the moment. I was always big for my age until I stopped at six feet, two inches. I was taller and stronger than my friends until the eighth grade when a few pals shot past me. I was a gentle, easygoing kid, but I knew the thrill of winning countless wrestling matches, sometimes against two or three at once. I tried not to gloat too much over my superiority, but the truth is it wouldn't have been too hard to teach me to kill for my country.

My family was casually patriotic. Both my brother and brother-in-law had been naval aviators or, as we joked, "nasal radiators." War songs were part of the repertoire at family barbeques, from "The Caissons Go Rolling Along" to "From the halls of Montezuma to the shores of Tripoli," leading into the peaceful harmonies of "You Are My Sunshine." And guns were commonplace. A .22 rifle replaced my BB gun when I was ten, and I'd been hunting ever since. I'd killed: animals, not people of course, but killed nonetheless.

As I grew up, war turned cold. I was two when World War II ended and, except for a distant disturbance in Korea, war itself had gone out of fashion and was replaced by our collective nightmare: the H-bomb. Whatever was going on in Vietnam, it wasn't as if someone serious like the Russians was threatening us. So my government's call to service was an inconvenience, something I was sure I'd avoid, even though some part of me felt thwarted that I wouldn't be able to prove my manhood in real battle.

The induction center down in Greenwich Village was crowded with apprehensive young men. We were told to strip to our underwear and carry our stuff from room to room. When I got to a doctor, he told me to put my clothes on the floor. He mentioned that I didn't seem to have any trouble bending over, barely glanced at the X-ray, and passed me on. I was informed that it could take as much as a year before the bureaucracy could again straighten out where to send the formal induction notice, but one thing I knew: My back wasn't going to keep my ass out of some place called Vietnam.

I wasn't dead set against this war, or whatever it was, but I was ambivalent. Until the Gulf of Tonkin "incident," Johnson insisted that there was no way America was going to war with North Vietnam. When it was mentioned at all, politicians insisted we were merely trying to peacefully help South Vietnam, this little outpost of democracy, stand up to some bad guys. Suddenly, magazines like *Time, Life*, and *Look* were filled with pieces that claimed that my country was trying to stop communism from spreading out of China, North Vietnam, and, yes, the Soviet Union. Newspapers reported that South Vietnam was a teetering domino, ready to fall under the evil sway of godless totalitarianism.

Although I was soon to meet many people who questioned my blind allegiance when I admitted it, it had never occurred to me that my government would lie. I'd grown up believing in God and country, terrified that the commies were going to drop an H-bomb on us. I couldn't have been more than nine when my friend Eric Williams and I volunteered for the Civil Defense and were sent up to the top of the tallest building in Palm Springs, California, our little town out in the desert. From that second-story rooftop, we ate Cracker Jacks and craned our necks for hours looking for Russian airplanes that the adults said might be coming to bomb us to kingdom come. I didn't really understand why they wanted to kill us, but we had a card with the silhouette of various planes to guide our identification of the bad guys. I didn't last long in the clutches of that degree of paranoia, but for a while it felt better taking action than waiting to jump under my school desk in case a siren warned us that a bomb was coming.

Over the years my political awareness had matured, if only a little. At some point I realized that the ultra-conservative John Birch Society was as dangerous, paranoid, and hysterical as a commie could ever be. By the time I got into college, I was as charmed as the rest of the nation by JFK and his classy wife. I felt inspired by the challenge our new president made in his inaugural address to "Ask not what your country can do for you, ask what you can do for your country." I was intrigued by his notion of saving the world through the Peace Corps, a very different kind of army. Even so, the Soviet Union was scary. They had tried to put missiles into Cuba in 1962, and it seemed like they were always trying to take over some country.

JFK's assassination in November of 1963 threw a blanket of fear and confusion over everything. Nobody knew who killed our president, unless you believed some little pro-Russia American punk could have pulled it off alone. That was hard to accept, and then to make it even stranger, some kook blew him away while surrounded by Dallas policemen. Chaos followed tragedy and we were all left to wonder who the enemy was.

Mostly I had been able to ignore politics. But seeing the look in the eyes of the guys who were being formally inducted that day of my physical shook me up. This was serious, life-threatening stuff, and I understood that some Army psychiatrist wasn't going to be impressed with a kid who was merely reluctant to go to Vietnam.

Confusion and depression over the draft, and questions about my sexuality, persisted until I decided I needed help—professional help. I went home to California that summer and saw Pierce Ommany, a psychologist who guided me into confronting my inner demons. He helped me personally, but back in Manhattan, I realized that one shrink's opinion that I was distressed and unhappy wasn't going to mean much to the Army. What I needed was a man with clout, and I found him in Dr. Ralph Dawson, M.D., Retired, Captain, Marine Corps. I figured my best chance was to get one military psychiatrist to convince another of how wrong I was for this job.

In the fall of 1965, I stayed busy with painting, life drawing, going to therapy, and a budding romance with Sigrun Mueller, a fellow artist. While I waited for my next draft summons, I talked at length about my situation with my neighbors, who got me to join the first big anti-war march, right down Fifth Avenue with 50,000 others chanting and shouting, trying to wake up America. I woke up to the fact that when 1965 began there were 23,000 American "military advisors" in South Vietnam, and it was estimated that by the end of the year the U.S. would have 185,000 combat troops in that steamy jungle. This was going to be a long war, and it wasn't just my ass they wanted.

The demonstration was the biggest crowd I'd ever been in, except for football games. Most of them seemed to believe that the U.S. government was not only lying but sinister enough to assassinate Diem, the president of South Vietnam and a supposed ally, and then install a new government more to our liking that would fight the commies in the north. Some of the marchers were like me, scared and ignorant. But others, like my "radical" neighbors, Nick and Joan, didn't seem surprised at what the government was doing. I wondered why they were so sure of what was going to happen in the world. I wondered if it had something to do with all the Marx and Lenin I'd seen on their bookshelves. I'd only read a little Marx in college, and Marxism in particular was blamed for damned near everything that was wrong in the world. But whatever the reason, so far, they were right.

One bleak winter day a letter arrived telling me to come in for my decisive physical. On March 2, 1966, I descended into the subway as if it were the first circle of hell and joined hundreds of other freaked-out guys for induction. Most of us lined up like sheep, but some explained to anyone who'd listen how or why they were going to get out. Being homosexual seemed to be a popular choice. A few were dressed as women or wearing bizarre outfits. There was a guy who explained he'd eaten two-dozen avocados that were going to push his blood pressure off the charts and cause him to be sent home. I never found out if the guacamole strategy worked. I had to go through the whole physical again. Then I was brought into a small office for a psychological interview because Dr. Dawson had sent a letter.

The Army psychiatrist leaned forward, his derision poorly masked. "What seems to be the problem?" Despite his cold, alligator eyes, I sincerely tried to answer. I opened my mouth but nothing came out.

I didn't yet fully inhabit the person who knew, coherently and confidently, the answer to that question. I knew that I shouldn't get into politics or try to explain that war, or at least this particular one, was wrong. I wasn't going to convince him that it represented nothing to die for unless it was blind obedience to a higher power: a government I'd never thought to question until it began sending guys like me six thousand miles away to keep dominoes from tipping over. I couldn't explain, wasn't yet aware of all its implications, that I'd already lived most of my life faithfully accepting an even higher power, God. The fact that I considered myself betrayed by Him for other reasons only added to my confusion.

I was quite certain that no one and nothing was All-Powerful, but that didn't erase the profoundly effective training I'd received to appease whoever was in control. I desperately wanted to answer the question, but I was so conflicted and confused that, try as I might, nothing came out. I tried again. My stomach heaved and my racing, flailing heart pounded. All that emerged was "I...I...I... " followed by strangled, partly formed words that sounded like the squawks and chirps of a dying bird. I wanted to explain that I wasn't trying to make trouble. I tried again, even willing to admit that that wasn't the complete truth, that my conscience, Catholic-trained and painfully sincere, was still convinced that I was just a weak coward trying to avoid responsibility. But, lips straining and brow furrowed, I couldn't form words, my moral compass swinging wildly between two poles while my pathetically earnest shuddering and yelping only underscored my lack of fitness to serve the cause. For nearly a minute he glared at me, until, with a slight shake of his head and disgust dripping from the corners of his closely clipped moustache, the man in brown put down *1-Y*, meaning that it was not currently worth trying to train me to kill other people. He didn't reject me outright with a *4-F* classification, leaving room for the possibility that the Army might be even more desperate for men in the future.

2

THE ORIGINS OF A LOVER

Now that I wasn't heading to Vietnam, I suddenly had a future. I decided to move back to California and get a master's degree in painting: The automatic deferment that graduate school offered amounted to a double indemnity against the draft. I had a lot of paintings to haul, so I needed to buy a car. That made me nervous.

I was an extrovert, a "people person," as my stepmom said. Some people thought I was handsome in a soft sort of way, and occasionally I reminded strangers of certain singers. A year ago an old guy asked me if I was Julius La Rosa, and recently a girl on the subway asked if I was Pat Boone. In general people assumed a big guy like me must be pretty sure of himself. I wasn't going to argue, but I also knew that it was something of an act. When I was nervous, I smiled a lot. When that wasn't enough, I became even friendlier. It had begun so early and become so automatic that I had no idea that I was trying to cover up any discomfort. On the contrary, it was something I did with such ease that I thought it was simply my nature. No one had ever accused me of being insincere, except once in high school. I figured that friend was jealous of me because I'd been elected class president. And even if being nice was false, it made others relax, so it did no harm. However, none of my natural charm was having an effect on the short, fat guy standing in front of me in an empty parking lot scattered with trash and broken blacktop.

"Ironically, my father was born here in Rockaway Beach or Far Rockaway or...something like that," I babbled through my grin.

The guy, Dorsey was his name, interrupted his counting and looked at me with a sour expression that indicated that irony held no magic for him. He gathered up the hundred-dollar bills and began once more to count them aloud. I was chagrined into silence, but in my head I continued with the story that my dad wasn't a New Yorker for long, that my grandfather had moved his family to California and they had homesteaded on the desert. While my inner monologue carried on, I nervously stood by, puckering and un-puckering my lips as Dorsey laboriously laid out the six new bills on the faded brown hood of the station wagon, and then scooped them up again with his short, hairy knuckled fingers and grunted his satisfaction.

"I made them myself last week," I joked.

Dorsey looked at me as though my humor was causing him heartburn. "Yeah, and this ain't my dearly departed mother's car. It's really a delivery wagon for dumping bodies off of Breezy Point. But it don't smell too bad."

With that he barked and showed off a missing tooth through his five-day growth. I stared at him: Ed Norton trapped in Jackie Gleason's body. Dorsey drew the pink slip out of the rear pocket of his grubby jeans and slowly, as if he were already arthritic at thirty-five, signed his name.

He handed it to me. "No returns, no complaints, right?"

"Right!" I confirmed loudly with false confidence, and shook Dorsey's meaty hand with enthusiasm. The deal was done.

Getting into the car, all I could think of was that I wouldn't have to pay the subway fare back into Manhattan. I was thrifty, that was no act. I'd been living on two hundred bucks a month, including seventy-five for rent on my fifth-floor walk-up, roach-filled apartment in Hell's Kitchen. Slowly, I was using up the money from a trust my dad had set up for my education. I was independently poor. So, for that moment, saving a quarter was more important than the six hundred bucks I'd just shelled out for this faded, crap-brown '58 Chevy station wagon. Six hundred seemed like a lot of money for an eight-year-old car, but it was the best deal I'd been able to find that offered me room for all my stuff.

Immediately I began to worry if the Chevy could actually make it across the country. I adjusted my rearview mirror and saw Dorsey walking away, his butt crack flashing above his jeans. I could feel myself lapse into second-guessing and what-ifs. The thought of trying to undo what I had just completed turned my mouth dry. I made myself ignore that voice and turned the engine over. It started without a hitch. I exhaled, hit the gas, and headed into the next chapter of my life.

Coming back into Manhattan over the Queensboro Bridge, my anxiety fell away. It was a beautiful June day, 1966, and optimism flowed through the open window. I got excited as I glimpsed the skyline that I had painted during my first year in the city, around the time I went for my first draft physical. An acting agent had come into the Art Students League looking for a student who could both paint and act for an industrial film, and a friend had recommended me. The guy cancelled the film or, at least, decided not to use me even after I had gone out and painted the view that they said they wanted. "Bastard," I murmured. It just confirmed to me what a ridiculous gig acting was. I was glad that I hadn't come out of college wanting to pursue that. Painting was hard enough, but at least I had something to show for a day's work. Still, it was enticing how many acting possibilities had cropped up, even though I hadn't pursued them. I'd stumbled into a month of *My Fair Lady* in Woodstock, NY, when I first came east in August of 1964. Summer stock hooked me up with a flock of struggling actors and singers in New York that first long, depressing, yet liberating year. In my second year in Manhattan, my new commie friends wrote a children's musical that I starred in. We performed in schools in Harlem and Lincoln Center. I was Red Beard the Prevaricator: The kids had to vote whether or not to send me to jail at the end of each show. I usually ended up in the slammer. I combed my fingers through my beard. I never cut it off after the show because Sigrun, who had become my girlfriend, thought it looked great. I twiddled with my moustache and smiled. It's too bad it was such a hassle to act professionally because doing theater was fun.

Dropping into midtown Manhattan, I made my way to West 57th Street. When a delivery space opened up in front of the Art Students League, I decided to take a chance on a parking ticket and pick up my last few possessions. I felt invulnerable.

The foyer was empty and even the office was quiet as I looked in. Classes were over for the day. I jogged up the stairs and found my box of brushes in Harry Sternberg's studio. A warm light filtered through the skylights. The smell of oil paint and turpentine lingered with memories of the paintings and students I had known. I'd stumbled in here with a BA in literature and a romantic desire to be an artist. Sternberg, a good friend of my dad's, had held out little hope for me at the beginning. He pushed me in his blunt, crass, New Yorker way to shit or get off the pot as I wavered in front of canvas after canvas. Showing surprising discipline, I slowly gave form to my feelings and ideas, and after two years, we both began to believe that I might actually have a painter hidden beneath my naive, friendly shell. Now I was headed back to California to get a master's degree in fine arts, full of a new confidence and bursting with ideas for the canvas.

Walking out of that room for the last time, I was glad that the place was nearly empty. I hated good-byes, and the final day of regular classes had been way too sticky sentimental for me. I poked my head into the lunchroom as I was leaving. Carlos, with his pock marked face and shifty eyes, called out, "*¡Hola amigo! ¿Qué tal?* I thought you had run off to California *sin decir adiós.*"

I winced guiltily. I had avoided Carlos and Tony on the last day of regular class because they had been such assholes. But at the same time, they were witnesses to many of the changes I had gone through in this place.

"Hey, Carlos, after all the *dinero* I've spent here, I thought I could at least get a free cup of coffee as a going-away *regalo*."

"Of course, *amigo*. I was going to throw it away since just about everyone's gone."

"Your generosity is exceeded only by your honesty, *cabrón*," I said with a laugh.

I continued chatting with Carlos in English salted with Spanish until he went to answer the phone. I sat with the strong Cuban coffee, listening to him rattle on in Spanish but not comprehending much. I recalled sitting in the cafeteria my first year while Carlos and Tony were laughing and calling another student "*maricón*" and "*buggarón*" behind his back. Even though I wasn't positive what the words meant, with a wink and a nod they drew me into their secret heterosexual cabal that sometimes formed when a "faggot" was spied. I tried to call them on it, questioning them as to how they were so sure. But they effortlessly turned it on me and began to call me those same names. I barely understood their rapid Spanish. When I tried to deny what they were saying, they only laughed at me. I didn't want to fuel their game by defending myself too vigorously and quit responding, but they took my reticence as agreement. They kept it up, teasing and taunting me off and on for the rest of that first year.

"Shit," I sputtered. Why hadn't I just punched out one of them? That would have stopped it. But that had never been my way. I never got that angry, never in my life lost control and took a swing at anyone. I was big but I preferred to talk my way out of conflicts. I prided myself on that ability, but I knew it made me vulnerable to guys who were more elemental: fuckers and fighters like Carlos and Tony.

I added some sugar to the bitter coffee. I had to admit that the teasing continued on for another reason. I hadn't been sure who or what I was sexually, and was too confused to argue either way. I was lost. When I finally confessed about feeling depressed and sexually conflicted to my painting teacher during one of that old radical's famous three-martini lunches, Sternberg urged me to get into therapy. The memory of that liquid lunch made me laugh, how blabbing my fears to a cantankerous Jew in a New York restaurant had replaced going to confession with an uptight priest. Still, I felt a lot better about that conversation than I ever did after confession—even if the advice hadn't worked out, at least right away. I sighed. That first shrink in New York was really a joke. He was a psychoanalyst whose idea of therapy was to silently sit behind me in a dimly lit room, expecting me to talk about my sexual confusion while he sucked on a burnt-out cigar. Wasn't that leading the witness? I laughed into my tepid coffee.

I looked over at Carlos, who had forgotten me completely and was into a dramatic harangue on the phone. My gaze wandered across the Formica tables and up to the old smoke-stained paintings hanging from the high walls. A portrait of some long-forgotten teacher from the League's past stared down at me with grandfatherly calm. I recalled the kind eyes and wild, graying eyebrows of Pierce, my therapist, who followed that character with the cigar. I'd returned for the summer to California and Pierce offered a space of "no judgment." Gently he encouraged me to observe my whirling mind: my thoughts and fears, my daydreams, night dreams, and fantasies. At first it was as if I were wrapped in a cocoon of fear. I'd lie on his couch, my eyes pooling with tears. I was filled with holes where feelings would have been if I'd not been so numb.

With my permission Pierce sat on the floor next to me, his head next to mine, and his arm across my chest. He was present, committed to taking this journey with me, not just impersonally observing me as if I were some performing animal. At first it seemed weird, but I was used to hugging: Everyone in my family was a big hugger, especially my dad. It was intimate but not seductive, sensual but not sexual. Pierce breathed in unison with me, and slowly I began to let go. He didn't say much. He simply bore witness, giving me support to release my control, to go into my fears, to trust myself. And so I began to give "reports from the interior" with Pierce sitting right next to me, his forehead leaning against my temple, just listening. We met twice a week for six weeks, and among many other things, I realized, almost guiltily since it had become such a big deal, that men didn't turn me on sexually. Hard-ons speak their own truth. Mine insisted, like the sailors in *South Pacific*, "*There ain't nothing like a dame!*"

At first I was like a lost, confused adolescent trapped in a man's body. I recalled being twelve years old in seventh grade, my first and only year of Catholic school. My parents had been divorced for over a year, and I lived with my dad. He knew the pain I was in and thought more religion might be good for me. Catholic school was okay. I made friends easily enough. Yet it also gave me the opposite of a "road to Damascus" moment. One afternoon, with school just over, I wandered into the church, waiting for my ride home. In a lonely silence I watched as sunlight streamed through the stained-glass windows illuminating the altar. Two kids, second or third graders, also waiting for their rides, came in behind me. A horn beeped. They shrieked and ran out of the church.

"Don't run!" I called out, and then whispered, "It's dangerous to be rude to God."

I turned back to the altar, ready to apologize for them, but it no longer seemed holy. It was just an empty room filled with sunlight. My mind exploded with a shocking realization: I can never be sure there is a God. With that thought I was transformed, exhilarated, ecstatic. I turned and flew out of the church. But it was short-lived. Quickly I was flooded by a wave of fear. It took me a while to find words for it, but finally I realized that the nuns in school had been right: Faith was a gift, an answer to the mysteries of life. I'd been given that gift at birth, and now I was thrust into finding different answers and never being sure.

It was a painful liberation, but I began to intellectually appreciate that belief in God was a choice rather than a preordained absolute. I was free to question everything. Yet the power and habit of belief doesn't reside in logic. Even though I began to prevail over Catholic dogma in theological debates carried on in my head, I discovered a priest had been implanted deep within my psyche, impervious to reason. Emotionally I remained terrified of Hell and all the things that would send me there: afraid to swear, afraid to kiss or touch girls, afraid to masturbate, afraid to challenge authority—afraid, afraid, afraid.

As I staggered through my teens, my fears began to weaken and I swore, masturbated, kissed, and felt girls up as I challenged the dogma, and myself. By twenty-one, nine long years later, I was ready to declare myself no longer a Catholic. I didn't go to church and, on most days, I didn't even consider the possibility of being condemned to Hell. At last I wasn't afraid to "go all the way" with Kathy Byrne, my girlfriend, who, like me, was a fallen Catholic. However, having wrestled the right to be sexual from the resident priest in my mind didn't mean I was sexually liberated.

In that short time with Pierce, I realized how deeply Catholic I had remained even after my faith had shattered. Just because I wasn't guilty over having an erection didn't mean I could behave in an adult, sexual way. Like so many of the priests I'd followed so ardently, I had been stuck in my early teens as far as my sexual development was concerned. This explained why it took so long to relax with a woman even after I had stopped believing that intercourse was going to send me to Hell. I had to grow up. It wasn't just premature ejaculation that was messing up so many sexual encounters that first year in New York: It was fear of myself as a sexual person.

My eyes snapped open as samba music suddenly filled the empty room from a little radio that Carlos had in the kitchen. I looked around and recalled when I came back for my second year, fresh out of therapy with Pierce. I had walked in with a new assurance, bought a cup of coffee from Carlos, sat down and romantically clicked with Sigrun. It put an end, once and for all, to their taunting.

I stood up. It also put an end to my fears that Catholicism was going to permanently scar me. My time with Sigrun had been too juicy and fun to leave any doubts about that. I saluted good-bye to Carlos, who was now dancing with a mop. I called out, "*Adiós,* you provocative piece of shit."

Unaware of my epithet, Carlos drifted out of his own fantasy and called, "*¿Dónde está su novia,* Sigrun?"

"*¿Mi novia?* She's no longer my girlfriend, *no más*," I shouted back.
"Too bad, *hombre*, she was good for you."

I was amazed and strangely touched that he had even noticed, but he was right. Furthermore, and as hard as it was to believe, Carlos and his taunting had been good for me as well. Like the draft board, he had forced me to get to know myself.

3

BLOWIN' IN THE WIND

I dropped off the Interstate just before I got to Indianapolis, and headed southwest on Highway 3 over to 46. Fields gave way to woods as small billboards announced that I was rolling through the Hills O'Brown in Brown County, Indiana. I could feel the tensions of New York slipping off my shoulders. Though I thought it somehow beneath me, like everyone I knew in New York, I had constructed a shell in order to handle the pressure of being on the streets of Manhattan. The whole idea of creating an invisible barrier to protect myself from the ongoing assault of the arrogant, the outrageous, the miserable, and the angry was new to me when I moved there in 1964. But as much as I hated to admit it, the streets were too noisy and the people too pushy and loud for me to handle with just a smile and courtesy.

Until then I had always trusted my personality to get me out of any tense situations, like when I was eighteen and my buddy, Weston Naef, and I drove down to the beach at Corona del Mar, California, and cruised into Merle's Drive-In in Weston's '53 Chevy with a big Chrysler engine squeezed in it. The new lime-green paint job glimmered under the polished chrome. Weston pulled into a parking spot next to a carload of locals, gunned the engine slightly and turned it off as the muffler rapped down, announcing the arrival of a badass machine. Sure enough, within a minute Weston was starting to argue with one of the guys in the next car about who had the more bitchin' hubcaps. Before I knew it, they had both jumped out of their cars into the parking, lot trying to provoke one another into throwing a punch. Four guys watched with eager eyes from the other car. Weston tended to go a little crazy at times, and I guessed that he would probably mess up the other guy badly enough that those others would be obliged to jump in.

My strong desire to not have to go to Weston's aid got me out of the car. With forced calmness, I walked over to the two guys woofin' at each other. They both paused as I approached because I was breaking up the space they needed for this part of the dance. I looked each one directly in the eye and asked with just the slightest edge of scorn, "You guys gonna fight over who's got the prettiest hubcaps?"

The tension turned into embarrassment and, with half-baked *fuck yous*, the two protagonists retreated. Weston and I got back in his car and ordered Cokes from the pretty blond waitress.

The memory made me laugh and want to get a soda. I pulled into a Texaco station in the little town of Gnaw Bone that had regular gas at 21.9 cents a gallon. A young, lanky kid with pimples and cigarettes in the sleeve of his white T-shirt filled it up, washed the windshield, and informed me that the oil was fine. I was starting to like my brown bomber. Drinking from the scarred green Coke bottle, I went into the pay phone booth and called my friend Mary Lindenstein in Bloomington, about twenty-five miles away. Just as she had told me when I'd called her from New York the week before, Mary was working on her dissertation while waiting for my call.

I'd known Mary since third grade. At some point in that year, I had kissed her but didn't make her cry as the rhyme predicted. Instead, she giggled and began to chase me. Now she was getting her PhD in sociology at the Kinsey Institute at the University of Indiana. She was a sexologist, which was more than a little intriguing. We had never dated in high school, and I hadn't seen her much during college. I'd always thought of her more like a sister, even though she was attractive and stacked. Since it took very little for me to spring an erection, I wondered what made the difference between girls who turned me on and those who didn't.

It took less than an hour of talking at Mary's apartment to discover that she had learned and experienced more than I had dared imagine. At twenty-four, I was still getting used to the idea that it was okay to have sex, while Mary was trying to get over a long-term affair with a married professor. I was rocked by various feelings: excitement at the idea of an illicit affair, sympathy for the pain of her disillusionment, and anger at some old married guy for leading her on. I told Mary about the older actress, almost forty but still good-looking, who was starring in the play in Woodstock that I was in.

"We became good friends and, when the play was over, she invited me to stay with her while I looked for an apartment in Manhattan. I knew that we could have had an affair—she even cracked once that some of her friends thought she was keeping me—but the only move I made was to my own apartment."

Mary shrugged. "What's important is that you had free choice."

I ached to have her nonchalance and lack of judgment. Even with all my changes in the previous year, I still had a sort of negative, Pavlovian response to sexual behavior that seemed the least bit immoral, like adultery. My reaction embarrassed me and I hid the part of me that judged her. It seemed to work. Mary didn't appear troubled by anything I said. She was caught up in her world where a man she loved was choosing to be with his wife. She felt foolish, that was judgment enough, and my apparent sympathy was all she needed.

After fixing dinner, we went to a coffee house, ordered beers, and listened to some folk music from a trio that was mostly rehashing Kingston Trio and Limelighter songs. I thought it was cool. It reminded me of when I was in high school and sang with my friend, Vic Pine, at a coffee house. It wasn't something many people knew, and when I whispered to Mary about it, she was surprised, saying that I seemed too square for that back in those days. She reached out and stroked my beard. "Did you ever hear Bob Dylan in Greenwich Village?" she whispered. "I just bought *Highway 61 Revisited.*"

I said no, feeling square again. I said that I was a jazz fan, and as the audience sang the chorus of "Kumbaya," I quietly but enthusiastically told her of my adventures in clubs in the East and West Village listening to Miles Davis, Rahsaan Roland Kirk, Yusef Lateef, John Coltrane, and others. Mary didn't know that music and wasn't impressed. I pushed on with my need to show her I was cool.

"My roommate and I used to put The Yardbirds on my record player, and on another turntable we put a round paper with patterns on it and stared at it as it turned while we smoked grass. It was pretty cool. It's called a light show. It's something they are starting to do at concerts, only it covers the entire wall of the place." Then I admitted, "I haven't been to any myself."

"I don't think that's made its way to Indiana yet," Mary said.

"How about marijuana? Have you tried that?"

Mary made a face. "I tried it twice, but the first time it just made me hungry, which I don't need." She laughed. "And the second time I felt strange and went to sleep." She shrugged.

The trio announced a break, and the room swelled with the sounds of conversation and a Joan Baez record.

"How about LSD?" I took a swig of beer.

"I've read a few studies, but it doesn't sound like it's for me."

I was about to admit that I hadn't tried it either when suddenly a big, bushy-haired guy sat down at our table with a clatter.

"Mary, how's it going?"

She gave him a peck on the cheek and introduced me as an old friend. "This is Jerry. He and I were lovers for a while as undergraduates, but then he fell for Karl Marx. I didn't have a chance after that."

She laughed as she said it, and Jerry turned to me and explained, "She's leaving out that she wouldn't return my calls for a month." He grabbed the waitress' arm as she passed and ordered a beer.

I absorbed how casual Mary was with an ex-lover and felt jealous, not just that Jerry had gone to bed with her, but because it was no big deal to either of them. "Is she right about the Marx part?" I asked, trying to get my mind off sex.

"Well, I wouldn't call it love," Jerry said, suddenly very serious, "because it's more than that." He lit up a cigarillo and exhaled into the hazy air.

Mary laughed a low, lusty rumble of a laugh, and I realized that under her current melancholy, a real woman had developed. I was intrigued and slightly turned on, but a little scared whether I could be a match for her.

"You see, Denny," Mary called me by the name I used until I was eighteen, "that was the competition I faced as Jerry fell under the sway of the communist plot to control the minds of the youth of America."

They started to debate the reasons for their falling out, and I sat back and realized that she had implied that there wasn't some sort of plot. All the anti-communist fears and slogans that had been such a part of my youth flooded into my head. How could she be so nonchalant about something that was such a big fear when we were kids?

After the waitress brought him a beer, I blurted out to Jerry, "What exactly does it mean to be a Marxist?" I was embarrassed to realize that I really didn't know what was involved. My college courses in political science and economics characterized it as an inefficient, totalitarian system. In that moment, only a few days after President Johnson announced we now had 250,000 troops in Vietnam trying to stop communism, it was obvious there was much more to it.

Jerry looked surprised to be asked such a basic question but threw himself into it. "Marxism explains, basically, why the government of a capitalist country like ours can never act in the interests of people like you and me. It's only going to do things that support and sustain the ruling class. Furthermore, the ruling class has opposite interests from the workers." As the implications of what he said soaked in, Jerry drank his beer and went on. "Being a Marxist means that you know you can't trust the power structure of this goddamn country, and you gotta do something about it before it sends you to war or buys your soul."

"I know that you gotta do something or you can get sent to war," I agreed, "but just because someone owns a company doesn't mean they're bad. Being rich doesn't automatically make you a bad person who wants to control everyone else."

"Name one," Jerry challenged me.

"Well, my dad, for one. He owns a company with fifty or sixty people working for him and he's fair."

"How do you know he's so fair?" Jerry asked and drank some more.

"Well, for one thing, I worked for the company three different summers, beginning in high school, and no one ever said anything about not being able to trust the so-called power structure."

"Gee, Denny, I wonder why they wouldn't have spoken to you?" Jerry said in mock confusion.

"Look out, Denny," Mary cut in, "he's a wind-up doll and you've wound him up. He will now be a completely arrogant shit until his spring wears out. He used to be divertible through sexual arousal, but that stopped working over a year ago." With that, she began to roar again and I, happy to be off the hook, joined in the laughter as Jerry challenged her to try again. But Mary waved him off, saying she wasn't interested in competing with Karl and Vladimir.

Jerry dismissed her with a comment that all women were teases. He turned to me. "This is why there are so few women who are leaders in revolutionary movements; they just don't get the big picture. They aren't able to conceptualize how to organize and change an entire society."

I laughed, trying to turn what Jerry was saying into a joke. I knew it was true that women weren't usually leaders, but I didn't know why and I didn't want to open up a whole new area for discussion with Jerry. I was still trying to figure out if maybe my father was part of the ruling class even if he was an ethical person.

Mary looked at Jerry with disgust. "The next thing you'll be saying is that all we are good for is having babies."

"And cooking and cleaning," Jerry added.

I signaled to the waitress for three more beers as Mary turned to me. "What do you think?"

I didn't want to take sides and offend anyone. "I'm just trying to find out what Marxism is, and suddenly we're having a war between the sexes."

"But," Mary persisted, "do you think women…"

"Leave your friend alone," Jerry interrupted. "He'll learn the true nature of this society as soon as he gets drafted."

"I'm not going to get drafted, not for now," I said, finishing my beer and feeling back on firm ground, "not that the sons of bitches didn't try."

"Denny, what happened? How did you get out?" Mary asked with concern.

"Did your dad pull some strings?" Jerry asked.

I looked away from Jerry. I felt a surging through my arms and shoulders and my jaw was tight. I composed myself before I looked him in the eye. "My father didn't have jack shit to do with me getting out of the draft." I hesitated because that wasn't exactly true, and I believed that I had to tell the truth. "Except he paid for the psychiatrist I saw for about six months, who then wrote a letter saying I wasn't psychologically fit to be in the Armed Services at this time."

Mary laughed and sighed simultaneously. "What he meant was that you aren't fit to kill people. Holy shit, Denny, that means you're so sane, you're crazy."

The waitress appeared, cleared away the empties, and left us with three cold ones.

Jerry grabbed one and leaned into me from across the table. "No, that means you bought your way out."

I blinked but didn't look away.

"Not that I mind," Jerry pulled back, "but let's call a spade a spade."

"You don't get it, Jerry," I said, angry but unsure if he wasn't right. "It was fuckin' scary. I didn't know what was going to happen until I went into the fuckin' Whitehall Street Induction Center for my physical and then was fuckin' grilled by the goddamn Army shrink, who wanted to know what my problem was. My ass was on the fuckin' line, man." I caught my breath and smiled, confident once again of how I had handled it. "The point is, the psychiatrist I went to was a retired Marine captain."

"Smart choice," Jerry nodded, "but chancy."

"Not like your endless student deferment, mister permanent graduate student," Mary shot back.

Jerry turned to me. "Do you notice how simple it is for women, since they don't have the draft to worry about?"

"I'm glad they don't have to worry about it," I argued.

"Hey, don't get me wrong here," Jerry said to us both. He pulled his long, curly hair tightly down against his scalp and quieted for a moment. "I'm for getting out of Vietnam any way a guy can, no apologies needed. But," and he released his hair, which sprang out again, and his voice recovered its volume, "we're also talking about the nature of American society, and Denny here is trying to argue that because his bourgeois father is a nice guy, we are somehow a classless society, and that's bull."

Mary looked at Jerry and shook her head. She leaned over to me and said, "You may notice that Jerry has become so revolutionary that he has decided to grow his short, curly, Jewish locks into some sort of natural to demonstrate his solidarity with black people."

"Screw you, Mary," Jerry said a little too loud to be ignored by the surrounding tables. "I suppose your little amorous adventures with Professor Sloan is all for your precious research?"

Mary's face went blotchy red and she quickly swept the room to see if anyone else had heard. "Jerry, if you're going to be such a loud-mouth prick, just leave."

The trio returned from their break and began tuning their guitars. Jerry took a long swig from his beer and stuck out his hand to me. "I trust I didn't offend you too much."

I took his hand. "You definitely stirred up some shit, but I did ask the questions."

"Well, that's what I'm here on earth for, to stir up shit." He finished off his beer, belched, tossed two dollars on the table, and turned to Mary. "I only say those things because I still care about you and I'm worried about you."

"I can only imagine what you'd say if you didn't care," she snapped.

The group broke into song as Jerry walked away through the smoky room.

I barely heard the music as I tried to figure out what Jerry was right about and where he was full of shit. I knew that not everyone could afford going to a shrink, so in some way I had bought my way out. But, hell, shouted a voice in my head, just because Dad could afford to help didn't mean it was wrong to do. Anyway, I told myself, my dad didn't really have anything to do with me getting out of the draft. I figured that out by myself. It was "chancy" like Jerry said, but I wasn't about to leave the USA and move to Canada like others had. I could live with what I had done.

I continued sipping my beer as the song ended. Mary was lost in her thoughts. I reached out and rubbed her neck and she turned and smiled. The trio announced a Dylan song and began before we had a chance to say anything. I fell back into considering the question of my father being part of the ruling class. That was harder to figure out. I knew my dad was fair. Everyone in town had always told me what an ethical man he was. But Dad did get rich from other people working for him; Jerry was right about that.

I looked around as the crowd joined the chorus of a song I'd never heard, *"The answer my friend, is blowin' in the wind, the answer is blowin' in the wind."* I dropped back into my thoughts, but soon my attention was snagged by a question in Dylan's next verse. *"Yes, and how many times can a man turn his head and pretend that he just doesn't see?"*

I remembered back to the summer I was fifteen, the first time I worked for my dad. I'd only been there a few weeks when I asked why there weren't any Negroes working there. He hemmed and hawed, but finally gave me a straight answer. "You know Fred, our general manager, and Albert, our chief engineer. Well, those two and about a third of the workforce are Mormons. Fred has made it clear over the years that they won't work with colored people, period. I've tried to change their minds, and several times I've hired Negro men as custodians where they wouldn't work with the regular crews. But somehow it always made trouble, and they never lasted for long."

I said it still wasn't fair and he hadn't argued. Instead he said, "This company wouldn't be able to run without the Mormons. What would you do?"

I didn't know the answer, but I guess my brush with the draft had suddenly made it clear that it wasn't enough to be a man of principle: You had to be a man of action. That could be intimidating. I looked around at the kids who were applauding and whistling and shouting out whoops of encouragement for the singers and the song they had just finished. I wondered how many of those guys were in school just to avoid the draft.

We drove back to Mary's apartment along quiet, tidy streets under a canopy of tall green trees. I answered her request for more details about the draft by describing how, three months earlier, I'd said good-bye to my girlfriend, Sigrun, and Duncan, my roommate, not knowing if I would ever return. "I'd heard they were in a seriously big hurry. Sometimes they put you in a bus and took you directly to basic training."

Once inside Mary's apartment, she turned to me. "My parents got divorced the summer after we graduated from high school."

"Jeez, Mary, I'm really sorry. I mean, I know how hard that is."

Her eyes filled. "I know you do, Denny. I guess that's why I told you, 'cause I remember how much your parents' divorce affected you when we were in sixth grade."

I felt an old sadness threatening to grab me and asked, "What happened with your parents?"

A few tears fell from her eyes as we settled down on a couch. "I guess all the usual stuff. They were unhappy with each other and sometimes they had terrible arguments. When Dad moved out, it was easier to see how bad it had been for a long time." She paused. "They hadn't had much of a marriage for years and…" She stopped but I stayed silent. "It turns out that my father is a homosexual." With that she stopped crying and looked at me with a "what can you do" shrug.

I was speechless. I couldn't imagine what it would be like to have a queer for a dad. It seemed impossible, yet here was Mary saying it was so, and that meant I had to find a place for it in my world. "Gosh," I finally croaked, "that's terrible." I could see from Mary's face that she wasn't sure if I was calling her father terrible. "I mean, it's really weird."

She nodded and looked away. I could feel I wasn't helping her feel better. "Do you still see him?" I asked.

"Of course," she said. "He's still my father."

I agreed with a big exhale. "Of course, yeah, sure." I realized that being a homosexual didn't have to be a problem. It wasn't even so unusual. "Remember when our drama teacher got arrested for propositioning some undercover cop in a bar?" I asked.

"I was one of the ones who started the petition for him to keep his job."

"Everyone in the class signed that," I said. "Both my dad and mom said it was okay as long as he wasn't messing around with kids. He was cool. I wish he'd been able to stay."

Mary nodded. "I never thought it would hit so close to home."

"Does your dad still live in town?"

"Until recently, but it's been hard." She looked at me again, her eyes showing that she was glad to be talking about it. "He got fired from managing the restaurant he had worked at for fifteen years."

"*Shee-it*," I said, "that's not fair."

"It wasn't for homosexuality," she said. "He was drinking too much…but that's better now. Anyway," she brightened up and tried to smile, "he's got a new job down in Laguna Beach."

I shook my head. "I'm sorry about all this stuff."

Mary gave me a warm smile and said, "Thanks, you helped me tonight."

I reached out and stroked her head with my hand, leaned forward and kissed her. She began to respond. I could feel her lips soften and her mouth open, but she pulled back as our tongues met. "I'm sorry, Denny. This isn't a good time for me to be doing this. I'm not ready to have sex with anyone while I'm still feeling that I'm in love with…" She sighed, "with a man who's old enough to be my father."

"I'm sorry to hear that too." I looked at her and cracked, "At least he's not gay."

She smiled. "Actually, that might make this breakup easier."

I sat wordlessly, trying to figure that out.

"Have you fallen in love yet?" she asked.

"Not love, but I was serious with someone, Sigrun, for most of this last year."

"How serious could it have been if it wasn't love?"

"I liked her a lot, but it wasn't fair to invite her to go to California with me if I wasn't ready to settle down with one person, and I wasn't. I…I…I'm not."

"Okay," Mary said quietly, "but the question remains, did you love her?"

My voice rose. "I don't trust love, so I never told her I loved her. I don't think it's fair to call what I felt 'love' because that would make it seem like it was going to last forever, and I know too damn well that nothing can make love last forever."

Mary put her hand on my shoulder. "Sounds like fallout from your nuclear family explosion."

"I guess so," I sighed, "but I like to think it's common sense too."

"Not that common," she said as she went to a closet and pulled out a sleeping bag.

"Funny," I continued, "I'm free to make love, but I can't declare love."

She gave me a sweet smile. "And I can admit I have loving feelings toward you, but I can't make love with you." She tossed the sleeping bag to me.

"Well, I can admit," I said, "that this is the most interesting time I've ever had not getting laid."

A giant insect with a bulbous head looked down at me, yellow eyes blinking with a cold curiosity. My heart began thumping, and I tried to calm myself by deciphering exactly what sort of beast was upon me. Suddenly its iron arms lifted a green metal box past its mouth, over its eyes, and threw it behind itself. Toby, my accomplice, did not stir from behind the steering wheel where he sat, similarly glued by a primordial fascination.

The screeching noise swung the whole scene into a more recognizable reality. With a jarring crash-thump, what had been the rapacious worm from the novel *Dune* transmogrified into a blinking, whirring, grinding dump truck on an otherwise quiet street at 3:00 a.m. in Columbus, Ohio.

"Far fucking out," I murmured, and we laughed. "My first time," I sighed, happy not to be holding onto any pretense. Toby laughed knowingly. I wanted to explain how perfectly everything fit together, but when I looked over at him, I could tell that Toby knew, and that made it even more perfect. I grinned at Toby, my new friend in the red T-shirt. He had driven us, like moths to a candle, to hover so closely behind the truck.

I turned back to the pulsing lights and whispered, "So this is psilocybin." It seemed like a long time since we'd first approached the garbage truck. For a long moment, I'd thought it was the cops waiting and worried if they could know we were tripping. I was glad I didn't have to explain myself to anyone.

Instead of words, I offered a big smile to the burly black guy who now appeared at the back of the truck, eyeing the two of us who had pulled up behind him on that otherwise deserted street with tired bemusement. "No need to be concerned, pal," I said and remembered what Toby had told me: "Psilocybin comes from mushrooms, used for thousands of years."

I whispered to Toby, "We are all children of the Universe." I felt a deep love for that black man, and I knew that this love was powerful enough to heal the tension and pain of racism. I knew from his kind eyes that he would understand why I didn't want to go to Vietnam. I knew this guy with the bulging muscles would understand my position because I was objecting to the war on behalf of everyone who was being taken advantage of in this society that had—almost overnight, it seemed to me—become mean and merciless and driven by greed.

I waved to him as Toby inched backward, then drove slowly around the garbage truck, wishing we could talk all this out but knowing my words wouldn't be able to keep up with my thoughts. Cut adrift from the necessity to explain, we glided effortlessly along that empty street. The soft caress of the early morning air coming through the window lifted me further into the truth of the sensation that everything was connected, divinely so, without effort, the whole universe in balance, the right amount of air, the right amount of light and dark, fire and water, soft and firm, huge and tiny.

We arrived at a house where we were supposed to be because Toby got out and walked slowly up the walkway. I didn't know where I was. I'd driven my station wagon in from Bloomington to visit Weston, my old friend with the long-gone, badass Chevy. Toby, another grad student, was there and offered to be our guide on a psilocybin trip. Weston took half of the sugar cube, but he just went to sleep as if it was dessert. My half sent me in a very different direction, and after a while Toby and I were…what? Going somewhere else where others were also tripping, and now we were there. It was simple and perfect and religious. I had already changed my beliefs, but now I was among millions of curious young people who were turning on and moving beyond the experiences and the religion of our parents. The velvety summer night was giving way to the dawn of new day in the middle of America on June 5, 1966, and I had just discovered a whole new world nestling invisibly inside the world that everyone could agree on.

I didn't know yet how painfully confusing it could be to come down and reenter a culture that didn't understand this experience and rejected it. I hadn't lived through times when there really were police behind those blinking lights. I had no idea how long the war was going to go on, or the price we were going to pay for it.

4

THE HOME FRONT

Radio KDES said it was 110 degrees as my trusty brown bomber pulled into the desert oasis of Palm Springs, California. I parked in front of the house where my mother and stepfather lived. I'd been driving for hours, but I wasn't ready to go in. I left the car running to keep the air-conditioning going. The deejay had Pat Boone crooning a bleached version of "Ain't That a Shame." Even I knew he should have been playing Fats Domino. But I had other things on my mind. I had faced some big challenges and gone through many changes since I'd been home. And I could no longer pretend that my parents' divorce hadn't devastated me.

I had been eleven, the youngest of the four kids, when they announced they were splitting up. The fact that my mother was divorcing my dad was devastating, but then she left me as well. Suddenly she moved a hundred miles away to Los Angeles with Jeanie, who was four and a half years older than me. My two oldest siblings, Gail and Jimmy, had already gone away to college, so my dad and I were on our own.

All of us kids were in shock: We had never seen them fight. Even Emily, our housekeeper, was surprised. Any kind of conflict, or just a heated argument, was rare, so we all assumed everything was fine. Mom told me she had tried to make the marriage work, but had been unhappy and "unsatisfied" for a long, long time. I was too young to understand the sexual component, but I believed her because the only other conclusion I could come up with was that she didn't really love me.

For the next two years, I saw her one weekend a month and a month in the summer. She offered to send me to therapy, but I said no; it seemed to me that the adults had the problem. I denied my pain by insisting that she had good reasons for leaving and deserved to be happy. Then, one day out of the blue, she said she was getting married again and asked me if it would be okay if she moved back to Palm Springs. I was thirteen. It felt strange to be asked since I hadn't had any power in the first place. I told myself I shouldn't complain because she was returning, and she really did seem happy. I was glad to have her back and kind of proud of her. When what she'd done got a name, "liberation," I realized I was an early feminist. But the damage was done, and nothing could truly fill the emptiness and confusion I felt in those years.

Now, fifteen years after she'd gone away, I sensed that her abandonment was like a deeply embedded piece of glass. Such a thick scar had formed over it that it was taking a long time for it to work its way to the surface. It wasn't out yet. I'd only recently begun to understand how her leaving had left me confused and exquisitely wary of trusting love.

I turned off my Chevy before the radiator boiled over. I'd grown up here and dug ditches in the summer when I was in high school, so I was used to scorching heat. But evidently living in New York had softened me up because as I pushed open the door, breathing was like sucking on a blowtorch. My stepdad's house lay shimmering in the heat. Mom had married Paul Summers, a Palm Springs high school teacher, and she'd moved into his house. Paul had come into this marriage with two boys, but Tony was already out of the house. I'd gained a younger stepbrother, PG, in this second family, but he wasn't there now. A quick glimpse at the roof showed me that the swamp coolers were cranking. I quickly went inside to find relief in the cool, damp air.

It was a pleasant enough homecoming until the three of us were well into our second gin and tonics. I turned to my mom on the couch and I mentioned with disgust that I'd heard on the car radio that three hundred U.S. warplanes had bombed North Vietnam that very day.

"Those red bastards deserve every damn bomb the B-52s can drop on their slant-eyed heads," Paul exploded from his easy chair. "They started this war and that's the only thing that'll get them to give it up."

I wasn't surprised he was pro-war, but his vehemence caught me off-guard. "How can you say they started this war when we have to fly six thousand miles just to get there?"

"Don't be dense, you know what I mean. They attacked us in the Gulf of Tonkin, and it's taken this long for that damn Johnson to fire back."

"Even if that were true, and I doubt it, why do you worry if a little country on the other side of the world goes communist? It's not our business."

"Because, unlike some in this country, I'm not a knucklehead who's afraid…" He hesitated. My mom worriedly pursed her lips. She'd been relieved when I told her about my successful battle with the draft board, but Paul clearly felt differently. I could see he was holding back from portraying me as a coward outright, trying to hang onto some vestige of family courtesy, but then he barged ahead. "You may not be willing to fight, but the whole damn world is our business, every nincompoop knows that."

"No, that's what certain people have been brainwashed to believe," I jabbed back. "Anyway, why don't you go over there and put your eager butt on the line instead of just cheering on the troops?"

"Stop!" my mother yelled, looked fiercely back and forth between Paul and me. "If you can't be civil, you can both leave and find dinner somewhere else."

Paul and I silently exchanged looks of anger and frustration, but he must have been salivating as much as I was from the smells of the lasagna that filled the house, so we both abandoned our principles long enough to eat in relative peace.

I stayed there off and on that summer. We went at it over the war whenever I was around, though we learned to avoid name-calling and instead flung facts and figures back and forth on the assumption that we could influence each other using reason. But it was clear that reason was just a front for some very strong emotions and presumptions.

Having sidestepped the war, at least for now, I felt a moral obligation to bring it to an end, and Paul was just plain terrified of appearing weak on communism. Back in 1964, he was a big fan of Senator Barry Goldwater, who was running for president against Lyndon Johnson. Goldwater wanted to give military field commanders in Vietnam and Europe the authority to use tactical nuclear weapons without presidential confirmation. In his workshop in the garage, Paul had engraved a wooden plaque with the Latin saying made popular by Goldwater: *Illegitimi non carborundum.* "Don't let the bastards grind you down." Now it hung in the TV room.

If our differences over Vietnam weren't enough, we found ourselves in an even more complex quagmire when we attempted to discuss race relations. Stokely Carmichael, president of the Student Nonviolent Coordinating Committee, which had been a vital part of the civil rights movement, had proclaimed "Black Power!" shortly after I came home. That threatening declaration became a staple on broadcast television. The face of civil rights was changing from that of determined but nonviolent black preachers like Martin Luther King, Jr., to younger black men, scathingly angry and increasingly prone to violence.

Paul was a teacher and a tough-minded disciplinarian. He insisted he was color-blind when it came to supporting and promoting students, and he had many letters of thanks and praise from ex-students of all races to prove it. But as much as he supported the hostilities in Vietnam, he had no tolerance for the destructive violence of angry blacks in cities across America that summer. When I suggested that black people had as much right to hate the "man" and fight back as the Viet Cong did to resist the Americans, he went ballistic. The perpetrators were "punks," "idiots," and, yes, "niggers."

One evening that August, we watched the news as Dr. King led a march for open housing in Chicago. Suddenly the marchers were attacked by a white mob, and MLK was knocked to the ground by a rock the size of a grapefruit. For some reason this riled Paul more than the white violence that had been fairly routine in the South for years. Yet he still blamed the protesters. "It's their own damn fault," he growled.

"Are you crazy?" I cried out. "How can you blame someone who was just about killed by a rock for throwing it too?"

Paul's face turned red and he yelled at me to turn off the TV. I was feeling more righteous by the second, and my mother looked ready to deliver another ultimatum to us both when, in the sudden silence, Paul put up both hands in a gesture of peace or "time-out."

"Let's all settle down. I've got something I want to tell you both." He paused. "I voted for Johnson in '64."

My mom was speechless, and I looked at him with deep suspicion.

"It's not that I liked him," he explained, "but Goldwater was such a hot-dog, jet jockey, ready to go to war in a second, that I was forced to support a Democrat."

I tried to look sympathetic but couldn't manage it.

"And there was another reason. After President Kennedy's assassination I knew someone had to get our country back on track. We had become a country governed by fear, not by law. So, I voted for the son of a bitch LBJ, and for a while I was hopeful. He whipped Congress into shape and passed the Civil Rights Bill in less than nine months. I decided I might have been right to trust a goddamn liberal."

"Honey, I never knew you were a secret Democrat," my mother said.

Paul scowled. "Well, you can forget it because it didn't last long… less than a week after that bill passed, the bill that was such a gift to the Negro people…"

"What happened a week later?" I interrupted.

"The Watts Riots! August 11th to the 17th, 1965," he replied, and then in a choked rage he spit out, "The goddamn niggers just couldn't wait. They couldn't play by the new rules that were finally in place, and they ruined everything."

My mom and I sat silent, shocked by the language and force of his feelings.

"And you better believe that I'm not the only one who turned against that so-called Civil Rights movement over those six days. Not only were those welfare frauds stupid enough to burn their community to the ground, but they did it on TV, for Christ sake. You can bet that every time another ghetto goes up in flames, a few million more white voters decide they've had enough of coddling those people."

"Now, honey," my mother said, trying to calm him. Then she added, "It is frightening."

"In 1964 that goddamn Johnson won by the biggest majority of any presidential election." Paul stood, too worked up to sit. "Voting for him was the biggest mistake I ever made. And burning down Watts and this Black Power bullshit are the biggest mistakes the Negroes ever made." He pointed at me as he left the room. "And you're too goddamn stupid to figure any of this out."

For seventy-five bucks a month, I found a storefront that had been converted to a big, open studio. Behind a high wall about forty feet back was a living space with a sleeping loft under a skylight, a tub, and a kitchen. The smells of oil paint and garlic mingled, and I loved it. I was two blocks from Wilshire Blvd., across the street from the East-West Cultural Center and around the corner from a halfway house for the mentally ill. MacArthur Park was five minutes in one direction, and I could make it to my classes at the University of Southern California in ten minutes in another direction.

My life as a serious artist in Los Angles began. I painted late into the night, entertained by deejays from "underground radio" like

Radio Free Oz on KPFK who concocted sonic brews as entrancing as a psychedelic. Something special was happening throughout the country. It seemed unique as well as a totally natural evolution of the human spirit and mind. Wherever I looked I realized I wasn't alone. More and more young people mocked the uptight, straight world, and when LSD was outlawed that October, it seemed like many simply laughed at the futility and hypocrisy of the U.S. government. Our drugs were banned while the Rolling Stones reminded us in "Mother's Little Helper" that tranquilizers like the ubiquitous Valium were being consumed like candy by millions who could only complain, *"What a drag it is getting old."* I could laugh at that, but then I played "Paint It Black," also by the Stones, as the evening news showed Blackhawk helicopters swooping over burning villages before dropping down to save our soldiers. Reality could be a real bummer.

It wasn't just the increasingly bloody war in Vietnam, race riots, and white backlash that were disturbing. Countries were testing nuclear bombs as fast as they could: the USSR at the end of September, France four days later, China two weeks after that, and the USA one week after that. It was obvious that there were a lot of crazy, scared people, and some of them were in charge of this world.

Culturally and politically I was becoming hip, yet it was all happening so fast that I also felt like Dylan's Mr. Jones when he sang, *"Because something is happening here, but you don't know what it is, do you, Mr. Jones?"*

Thanksgiving came around, and instead of going to the traditional family celebration, I said I wasn't going to sit around while everyone acted like everything was all right when so much was screwed up. It wasn't just the larger world that was messed up by war and racism; I was tired of the family ignoring strong emotions about damn near anything and, in particular, I was no longer willing to pretend that everybody was getting along fine in the wake of our parents' divorce.

When they divorced, my parents announced that we would still maintain some "family" traditions like celebrating the holidays together: Christmas, Easter, and Thanksgiving. Somehow they made that work between them, and after they each remarried, our stepparents and stepbrothers joined in. By 1966 we'd become a pathetically jolly extended clan. It was supposed to be healing, but for me it reopened a wound every time we gathered. When I saw my parents together, what I observed was that they had much more in common with one another than they had with their new mates. Mom and Dad shared an interest in art and books and had similar live-and-let-live philosophies. They were open-minded and curious about ideas and people. In short, they were innately prepared for the explosion of changes that were engulfing the society. Why the hell weren't they married? And who were all these other people?

So, as November approached that year, I decided that I couldn't stuff my feelings for another turkey dinner. I returned to my mom's house for the vacation, but I told whoever wanted to know that I thought the extended family gatherings were hypocritical and, instead, I went to some friends' house. Emotional outbursts were unknown in my family, and my small gesture of unhappiness and defiance was dismissed as "a phase" if it was discussed at all. My mom said that she missed me but otherwise avoided a deeper conversation.

As I was packing up to return to LA on Sunday, she came into my bedroom and gave me a thick, worn book with gold lettering on a scarred red cover: *The Awakening of the Desert*. It was a memoir of crossing the country on horseback and covered wagon in 1866 by Julius Birge. Birge was her maiden name.

"He may have been your great-great-great uncle, on my father's side. He was the first white child born on the frontier in Whitewater, Wisconsin," she said, "around 1840."

She never explained why she gave this to me rather than to my siblings, and I doubt she appreciated the irony of giving a gift in that moment that emphasized family connection. Nonetheless, I think she had a premonition that it would eventually have a strong effect. In her Unitarian, no-nonsense way, she was very intuitive, very in tune with the notion of human awareness being part of a universal mind. Her own spirituality was less apparent while she was married to my dad. Like all non-Catholics, she had to sign over religious training and the well-being of her children's souls to the Catholic Church. That was the price that the Pope extracted for intermarriage in those days, and she didn't challenge it. However, in the years following the divorce, she often spoke of "archetypes" that were shared within our "collective unconscious." Both were core principles of Mom's favorite psychiatrist, Carl Jung. She had been in Jungian analysis to give her the strength and self-acceptance to leave her twenty-year marriage. It worked and set her on a new path.

However, after my own experiences with therapy, I was beginning to sense that it didn't get at certain issues from her childhood. For example, family lore had it that her father—Gramps to me—was a moody, excessive drinker in his early years. There were stories about him breaking the fine china with explosive anger but no one challenging him either during or after the episodes. By the time I knew him, he'd been reduced to a small, rotund man allowed only one "snort" before dinner. He was fairly deaf and hard to know. I'd guess he was never the sort to encourage conversation or snuggling from a little kid.

One of three kids, Mom grew up the favorite of her heavy-drinking, carousing dad. Even though it didn't apply to my parents, I'd learned that growing up with a drunk could make a child hyper-alert and aware of threatening changes in behavior before they even happen. It's a survival skill, but it also teaches one to never get too close, especially to someone you love. My mom was caring but cool, with some part of her always kept at a distance. It seemed to be her nature. Maybe it was. She always said that she was an introvert, but I had a sense that her father's bourbon-soaked capriciousness reinforced it more than she knew. Of course, none of this was mentioned.

I thanked her for the book. I was young and living in very exciting times. We were making history, not studying it. The distant past didn't seem all that relevant to me, and family history in particular seemed boring. More to the point, this gift seemed like a way to avoid talking about my Thanksgiving boycott just like everyone in the family sidestepped talking about most uncomfortable subjects. Still, I took a risk and addressed an issue that had been weighing on me.

"Mom, are you happy?"

She looked surprised by the question, then recovered and said, "Of course, I am. What...?"

"Mom, I see when you get upset with Paul...like this morning at breakfast when he was practically crowing about Reagan being elected governor before he got into lambasting psychiatrists for trying to excuse the student protests in Berkeley."

She looked thoughtful and would have answered, but I jumped in and asked the question I'd been holding back for years. "Mom, how can you stand to live with him?"

Her lips tensed...and she walked out of my room.

I sat for a while, stunned but not really surprised at her response. I felt a little guilty. I'd gone too far. I'd put what I wanted into the form of a question, and it wasn't surprising she wasn't ready to deal with it. I went into the TV room, interrupted Paul and PG watching a football game, and said good-bye.

My mom followed me out to my station wagon. She looked at me with a mix of love and defiance. "Paul is a good man. You're old enough to realize that no marriage is perfect. We have our differences, but I decided that I was going to make this work." She smiled. She was happy enough.

I nodded and felt compassion for her. She wasn't going to go through another divorce, and she most definitely was not going back to my dad. She handed me some homemade chocolate chip cookies for the drive back to LA and gave me a hug good-bye.

I hugged back and realized that my compassion was also for me. Once again, I had to learn how to live with her choices. Unlike when I was eleven, I felt ready.

5

MAN OF THE YEAR

TIME magazine started 1967 off with a bang by naming me "Man of the Year." Well, specifically, it was men twenty-five and under who were so honored. I was twenty-five. They said we were a new kind of generation that was going to "land on the moon, cure cancer and the common cold, lay out blight-proof, smog-free cities, enrich the underdeveloped world, and no doubt, write *finis* to poverty and war…" They added, "Today's youth appears more deeply committed to the fundamental Western ethos—decency, tolerance, brotherhood—than almost any generation." They went on to invent a word, omphalocentric, to suggest we were overboard in our self-centered navel gazing, but, nonetheless, "he stalks love like a wary hunter, but has no time or target—not even the mellowing Communists—for hate."

I was torn. Even if it was coming from an establishment rag, it was hard not to agree and take it personally. In spite of being suspicious of their motives, having others confirm that what I sensed was novel if not revolutionary made it more real.

The thing that had always driven me crazy about adults was their hypocrisy: They said one thing and did another. Catholics had sex outside of marriage. Drunks lectured against marijuana. And the President bombed civilians to make peace. My generation may have been breaking laws, but we did it for a principle, openly. Dylan said it best in "Absolutely Sweet Marie": *"To live outside the law, you must be honest."* We were such good citizens that we broke laws in order to protect our constitutional rights, like demanding "free speech" at UC Berkeley. We publicly stood up to racist laws, warmongering draft boards, and other rules that tried to control our behavior. All Governor Reagan could say was that we were commies and riffraff, but obviously, many adults were paying attention, and a lot of them agreed with and admired us. Every day more and more people of all ages were calling out our government for lying about the war. And we were doing it peacefully. Even the part of my generation that had heeded the government and had gone to fight in Vietnam began to publicly question the war. Alongside these returning Vietnam veterans against the war another movement took the stage, "The Resistance" to the draft. They counseled and supported the boys who wanted to burn their draft cards. A kid was no longer as isolated as I was when he tried to figure if he should split to Canada or endure the potential five years in jail if he refused to serve. Lots of young men were proving their manhood by not going to war.

What did the Establishment gain by complimenting this huge upswell that I was part of? Maybe they meant it. There was increasing evidence that some of the so-called "grown-ups" were beginning to think we were right. Millions of Mr. Joneses were waking up to what was happening, changing just like I had. *Put that in your martini, Paul!* I thought.

The biggest fucking change, literally, was the Pill. That was all you had to say: "The Pill." It was like there were no other kind of pills. It seemed to show up about the same time that I decided that sex wasn't going to send me to Hell. Serenfuckingdipity! It took a few years for young women to get comfortable with the Pill and for me to get used to casually having intercourse. But now it seemed we were all on the same page, and it was a very fine thing indeed. Not that I didn't have to get used to the idea that girls were as interested in sex as I was. My friend Mary was but one example of the new attitude. The Pill served up sex without unintended consequences or hypocritical rules, and it changed the mating dance around the world. It was the Pope's nightmare, which only added to my pleasure.

I met Mavis at USC in a Renaissance art history class. She was a sculptor raised in LA. She was West Indian, Jewish, and, at twenty-eight, an older woman. After class one night I invited her to a party at a commune near Lafayette Park, not far from my studio. The commune took up the whole second floor of a commercial building, a big, wide-open space with curtains here and there creating somewhat private rooms along the walls. We smoked hashish and danced with twenty or thirty others amidst swirling colored lights to Jefferson Airplane, Aretha Franklin, The Beatles, The Beach Boys, and more. After two hours of this energetic foreplay, we walked the few blocks to my studio, hugging and laughing. I began to undress her from behind as she stood admiringly in front of one of my paintings. When her last garment fell to the floor, she spun out of my arms and pressed me against a wall. Slowly, she proceeded to undress me; then she took a dry paintbrush and brushed all over my body. My goose bumps had goose bumps. Then, with a leisure surely born from experience, she gave me my first blowjob.

Not much later I kept to the oral theme of the evening and reciprocated on Mavis' inviting mound of Venus, another first. Mavis and I fucked and reloaded and fucked some more in a crazed, animal state for the rest of the night. It was different than with Sigrun and other women. It was pure sex. My body resonated to the overwhelming power of a liberated energy that seemed like it could devour the world. Carnality! I had a profound, tangible sense why the Catholic Church had worked so unrelentingly at locking up the sex drive or, if that failed, harnessing it to marriage. Sex was revolutionary. You could lose your mind in it, or find God. Either way, it was a threat.

The next morning I lay in a hot bath as Mavis slept. My dick had never been happier. There was no guilt to ruin my high, but I couldn't believe how stupid and weak I'd been to believe the Church's line about sex. I began an inner rant about how naive and simplistic Catholics were and then stopped. I was blaming the sinner, myself included. That had to stop. The thing about the Church was that it made you ashamed of all sex. It wasn't just gay sex or whatever other people might say was wrong. All sex was wrong before you were married, and you could go to Hell forever if you didn't admit it was wrong and ask—no, beg—for forgiveness. To take this seriously was to be driven to madness by your desires and needs. I knew too well that repression scarred a person in ways that didn't show up until he tried to be sexual. Yet, in spite of this soul-sucking brainwashing, I'd finally reached manhood.

Into my self-congratulations crept the thought that this was why Paul satisfied my mother. Immediately I understood that though I couldn't stand him, I couldn't completely write him off. He gave her what my father hadn't, or worse, couldn't. I recalled the sadness that leaked from my mother when she talked about the divorce and her unhappiness. I knew my parents had both been virgins and their sex life was severely limited by the fear of getting pregnant. Dad had never had the chance to become an adventuresome lover. He was a captive of the Church and he hadn't broken out. Even though I couldn't be sure of all this, it felt true and I knew now more assuredly than ever that it wasn't going to be my fate. I wondered if Dad had discovered this version of heaven since the divorce. I hoped so, but I didn't see how I'd ever be able to ask.

Later, after some leisurely "good morning" sex, we walked back to get our cars and dropped into the commune, where we had tea with my friends Warren and Heidi. Warren told Mavis how they'd worked out an easygoing living arrangement. People shared in everything. Decisions required a consensus, not just a majority. Warren, a successful graphic designer, explained that those who worked put in money for rent and food, and others tended to the cooking and cleaning.

Heidi added that there was no ownership of any kind, and that sexual arrangements were loose. "Whatever feels right." She smiled. "You know the saying, monogamy equals monotony."

Mavis noted that since the men had the good jobs, the whole arrangement was actually quite traditional: women in the kitchen and the bedroom. *So what?* I thought, while Heidi said, "It's different since everyone's free to choose."

"Personally, I think of us as similar to the Essenes at the beginning of Christianity. We're part of a collective change for these times," Warren said with an air of warning. "But it only works if it's happening at an individual level."

Heidi turned to us and said, "Two weeks ago we went to this huge celebration in San Francisco, a 'Be-In.' It was so cool. There must have twenty or thirty thousand people, with most of us on acid and grooving with each other for the whole day in total peace and love. If it wasn't Eden, it was Heaven." She giggled and added, "It's like some professor guy said on the stage: Once we turn on and tune in, we can drop out and create a whole new society."

"Timothy Leary," Warren said, "and it's bullshit. It takes hard work."

Heidi leaned over and tried to kiss him on the cheek, but he pulled away. "Warren's a little freaked out that things will get fucked up if people flake out and only try to imitate those of us who are really into raising our consciousness."

"You aren't hip if you try to be hip," Warren warned.

Two more denizens emerged from a curtained nook. I recognized Angie, who lived there, and she introduced us to her new friend, Franklin, a small, muscular man. Even stretching and yawning, clearly just waking up, there was something intriguing, if not a little intimidating, about him. He was older with a little goatee and an unruffled cool about him. "Well, won't you look what a fine collection of cats and kittens we got here," he said as he approached. Then I realized this cat was a beatnik.

"You folks seen Rondo this morning?" Franklin asked in a silky baritone. No one had, and he turned to Mavis like she was an old friend and explained, "My son's been living here for two months, since he got out of the joint. Good kid, but not as smart as his daddy." He winked. "He got caught."

"What did he do?" she asked.

"Stupid shit, burglary...got six months for it. Should straighten him out." He coughed and turned to Angie. "Baby, be a doll and get me some mint tea and a little honey."

Angie skipped off as he sat down.

"You couldn't straighten him out on your own?" Mavis prodded him.

He cleared his throat with a low rumble. "That's about the only thing I couldn't do. Woulda been more trouble than it was worth."

"Meaning?"

"You're persistent." He sighed and stuck out his hands into the center of the circle we'd formed. They had more scars, swollen knuckles, and all-around wear and tear than any hands I'd ever seen. "One hundred and twenty-four professional fights, my sweet interrogator. Lost only nine and those were when I was younger, before I learned how to protect my handsome face." He smiled and revealed a couple of spaces where teeth had once been.

"So?" Mavis said, trying not to sound impressed.

"So these are deadly weapons and couldn't be pressed into an educational role no matter how badly the boy needed to be taught." He shrugged. "Anyway, I'm retired. I'm a lover, not a fighter."

Mavis cocked her head. "I imagine you've got scars from that as well."

Franklin let out a raucous laugh and looked over at me for the first time. "I like this chick."

I chuckled with him. "There's a lot to like."

Mavis looked at her wristwatch. "Don't any of you bums ever work?" she cracked as she scribbled something on the back of a matchbook and tossed it to Franklin just before Angie returned with the tea. She leaned into me and wet-smacked me, tongue and all. "See you in class, big guy," she said and headed for the door.

I told myself not to be surprised that I would soon be replaced. Sexually, Mavis was a Formula One Porsche and I was a '48 Chevy coupe just getting out of first gear. I'd already figured out that we didn't have a future as a couple, but I was hoping we could drive around a few more times.

I got up and went to the head. When I came back Warren and Franklin were discussing the existence of God and sharing a joint. I begged off. I planned to paint if I could stay awake after that sexual marathon. Franklin walked me to the door and asked, "Can I assume you're cool with me calling Mavis? I figure we might all show up here at some point, and I like to avoid bad vibes if I can."

"Sure," I said, "thanks for asking."

It was strange. I felt jealous and relieved. I'd just enjoyed something profound with that woman, something naked, vulnerable, and wild. And now I was agreeing to share this with Franklin. It didn't matter that I really didn't have a choice. The fact that we could share this woman's passion created a new sort of brotherhood, one beyond competition and ownership. I'd never believed that was possible. Liberated sex for sex's sake opened up a lot of doors.

I was halfway down the stairs when I remembered I was out of brown rice. I returned and borrowed some from Sunshine, another member of the commune. When I had met her in the fall, she had encouraged me to get on a macrobiotic diet, and brown rice and vegetables were the basis of it. It was supposed to be good for you in a dozen different ways, but you had to cleanse your system, including giving up alcohol, if you were going to do it right. That was okay with me. My family treated cocktail hour like a religious obligation, but I could do without it fine.

"I'm going out to the desert next week and I'll get a hundred-pound bag from Hadley's, along with another five-gallon can of honey," I told her.

"You're looking great, Dennis, the pounds are just dropping away." She gently pinched what was left of the fat tire around my waist.

"Lost almost twenty pounds already," I said. "I think I'm down to 175."

"Mmm," she purred. "Long and lanky: I may have to see you naked."

The truth was she didn't turn me on, but that seemed cruel to say. "Sorry," I blushed, "but you look way too much like one of my sisters, and I don't think I'll ever be liberated enough for incest."

"I can dig it," she said, "we can just be family," and she seemed sincere. "Actually, it's kind of a relief."

I wasn't sure what she meant but I was too tired to ask.

I headed home thinking that the Pill overthrew the convention or, as Mavis called it, the patriarchal myth, that women didn't have a sexual need and desire equivalent to men. Sexual liberation meant that many, not all, but many women I met were "turned on" in general. It was like they had switches all over their bodies and minds. Some were still a bit dazed and confused by it, but others, like Mavis, weren't embarrassed in the least as they moved through the fields of potential partners, harvesting at will. She certainly wasn't unique in enjoying anonymous romps as much as any man. It may have been the residual Catholic in me, but this seemed an even greater challenge to the status quo than Marxism. After all, was there a country in the entire world where women were accepted as equals to men in terms of lust and permitted to act on it? Not a one that I knew of, though it appeared the USA was headed that way. Men, myself definitely included, enjoyed this turn of events. But most guys I talked to about relationships still wanted an "off switch" once they got married. Traditionally that was known as monogamy and it had also traditionally been applied to wives more than husbands. I was in no hurry to get married, but I could see there was going to be some hard bargaining in the future if everyone was going to be honest about sex.

6

CULTURE WARS

Without trying to or planning it, I found that my personal changes were in sync with an evolving cultural awakening. Some people thought we were saving, if not reinventing, our country. Others called us pinkos, perverts, and freaks. I'm sure the majority thought we were some kind of crazy. However, craziness itself was being redefined. Psychiatrists like R.D. Laing insisted that we treat schizophrenics and other mentally ill folks more humanely, and people were listening. In a rare political agreement, liberals and Governor Reagan honored the civil rights of thousands of long-term mental patients who'd been inappropriately committed to psychiatric hospitals by releasing them. Soon, more and more of these folks found themselves in community-based homes. Reagan loved saving the state a lot of money, and liberals and psychiatrists loved redefining "normal." By chance, I was in the middle of that radical change too.

As I've mentioned, my studio was near an outpatient home for patients recently released from Camarillo State Mental Hospital, so I had several interesting visitors knocking on the glowing, frosted glass windows of my storefront as I painted late into the night. Celine tapped lightly one night, curious about what was going on behind my door. She could hear Thelonious Monk playing inside and wanted to tell me about another brilliant pianist who'd been in Camarillo with her. She entered cautiously and looked around very respectfully. She was middle-aged, small, and a little plump. Her face had deep lines, yet her olive skin was smooth between the lines. I asked the name of her friend, that maybe I had him on an album.

"Nope," she said in a firm but gentle voice. "It's up to him to tell you when he gets out. Hard enough to make a living playing jazz without people knowing you crazy too." She added, "But he used to play for the patients."

"They had a piano inside?" I asked.

She nodded. "They let him play occasionally, but even when they wouldn't, he'd play on the table, humming and singing the music." She smiled at the recollection. "Most everyone calmed down better with that than with the drugs. Course Snap never thought he needed drugs, never thought he was crazy."

"Snap?"

"That's what we called him…'cause he was always snapping his fingers."

At my invitation, she sat down for a cup of tea and some banana bread. We had a meandering chat for a while until she got down to what she evidently wanted to discuss.

"I hear the governor is going to let lots of folks out pretty soon. Says he's going to save the taxpayers money and 'depopulate' the mental hospitals, even those worse off than Snap and me."

"I read about that. It's great," I said. "Seems like the Republicans and Democrats can at least agree that people shouldn't be involuntarily locked up for years."

She snorted derisively and asked, "Sounds good, but who do you think will take care of them?"

"Community homes, like where you are," I said.

"Maybe, but that takes a river of money. If that dries up, we're all going to end up floundering on the streets." She peered into an unfocused future. "What I see is a lot of people without help or a home."

"But that would be cruel and self-defeating," I blurted out. "Really stupid."

Celine stared at me like the sphinx. I absorbed her silent wisdom and finally said, "That's a pretty bleak assessment."

"I get pretty dark sometimes, depressed. It's driven me inside twice. It's like the whole world is like a spider web and I feel it whenever it jiggles." She looked at me with dark, sad eyes. "Doctor says that too much sympathy can drive a person crazy. He calls it 'terminal empathy'." She sighed. "I told him that I'd rather be crazy than not feel it."

"Tough choice," I suggested.

"Not really," she replied.

"Not really a choice, or not really tough?"

Her eyes went to the ceiling in thought and she said, "Both, I guess." She went quiet, looking at my paintings, especially four big abstracts, similar in style to Franz Kline and a bit of Hans Hoffman. When she finished her cup, she said, "I like your paintings. I can feel you in them. Powerful, hopeful."

She thanked me for the company and walked back into the night, leaving me with one of the most important compliments I ever received.

I didn't go home for Easter, boycotting another family gathering. Instead I went to the first Love-In in Los Angeles in Griffith Park, with around 25,000 dancing, tripping others. Great music and mediocre marijuana were everywhere, and I returned home from a long afternoon of dancing and picture-taking with beautiful, bright Beth Markowitz, whose alabaster skin glowed beneath shimmering black hair. She was nineteen, a student at Los Angeles City College, and still living at home. When we finally came up for air after three days of deep immersion into one another, she called her parents to say that she was moving into a studio with a tall, lean, longhaired painter. I had become what was beginning to be called by straights and the media a "hippie," but labels were a turnoff. Rules and assumptions were breaking down and who knew what it all meant. Nonetheless, I still had to meet the parents. They wanted to know who had seduced their daughter and where she'd been.

When you've been raised to believe that you can go to Hell for having sex, it's mind-blowing to find that other people couldn't care less. I discovered that Jewish parents, at least these ones, weren't worried about "living in sin." They simply wanted to know if I could support myself—very practical. They didn't demand particulars, but learning that I was at the USC working for a Master of Fine Arts degree was reassurance enough. I was an artist, so even my long hair and beard made sense.

Beth brought a suitcase, took over a corner in the back, and, quite suddenly, I had a live-in girlfriend. I fucked, painted, went to classes, came home, drew Beth naked, and had more sex. I was living the Cultural Revolution and it felt as natural as growing my hair longer and longer.

As spring unfolded, LBJ kept saying we were winning the war. He continued to bomb North Vietnam, all the while insisting he was avoiding civilians and working for peace. Occasionally he offered to stop bombing as "an incentive" for its president, Ho Chi Minh, to give up. But LBJ always added that North and South Vietnam would have to remain as separate countries. It was a sham of a negotiation, and Ho told him to remove his 340,000 troops and his bombers and "let us settle our own affairs." Even though we were supposedly winning, General Westmoreland—our military leader whose name was an irony in itself—said we needed 200,000 more troops if we wanted the war over in two years instead of five. Two years? Five years? This nightmare was threatening to last forever.

Out of a steady stream of military, racial, and cultural crises emerged an inspiring union: Nobel Peace Prize winner, Martin Luther King, Jr., joined America's favorite pediatrician, Dr. Benjamin Spock, for a walk through Manhattan with 200,000 people right behind them in the largest anti-war march to date. Eleven days before, on April 4, 1967, Dr. King, against the advice of his supporters, had come out strongly against the war, calling for defeat of "the giant triplets of racism, materialism, and militarism." The civil rights movement and the anti-war movement were united once and for all.

For two decades, the author of *Baby and Child Care* had instructed our parents how to raise a child, and he'd long decided that nuclear weapons and this war were bad for us. His critics claimed he was responsible for this whole cultural conflict by insisting to post-World-War-II parents that "what good mothers and fathers instinctively feel like doing for their babies is usually best." Be flexible and affectionate, he said, and treat kids as individuals. He followed this up with the assertion that children, rather than requiring harsh discipline, would direct themselves into adulthood by following their own common sense. That's just what we were doing, and it was freaking out a lot of supposed adults. Critics complained that without proper discipline, we were addicted to "instant gratification." It became another argument that went around in circles.

In response to this massive anti-war protest, Secretary of State Dean Rusk appeared on *Meet the Press* to convince people that "the Communist apparatus" had organized the protests. Our government was lost in the 1950s, trying to make the case that we were "dupes" in order to rationalize its attack on North Vietnam. Around the same time, on another channel, boxing champion Muhammad Ali declared, "Man, I ain't got no quarrel with them Viet Cong," and refused the draft. It was hard to know who was winning in Vietnam, but the culture wars seemed to be going our way. Even the Supreme Court saw the light and finally prohibited laws against interracial marriage. Certainly, our warmongering government was struggling to keep up. You could smell their fear. But for me, and millions of others, the sense of things coming together was far stronger than the feeling that things were falling apart.

I had to sell the Chevy station wagon, my old brown bomber. Bringing me safely to California had about worn it out, plus it was too small to cart around the big canvases I was painting. I bought a new VW van, took out the seats, built in a sleeping platform, and still had room for my art. I loved driving around town listening to the Byrds' "Mr. Tambourine Man" pouring out of the radio.

Both hope and dope were in the air on Friday, June 16, 1967. The Beatles had just released *Sgt. Pepper's Lonely Hearts Club Band*, and everyone I knew immediately recognized this album as ours: a multifaceted, rocking emblem of the times created by turned-on minds tuned to our collective wavelength. Inspired, Beth and I headed up the California coast in my van to see and hear the Monterey Pop Festival with Mike Murphy, an artist and photographer who'd been showing me how to print photos in a darkroom. If a new way of living and being was entering the imagination of the American psyche, then it was music that was gluing the parts together.

That evening we pulled into the Monterey County fairgrounds as Simon and Garfunkel were serenading everyone from the fenced-in concert area. Their harmonies flowed through the oaks as we set up our tent. There were thousands of others settling into a scene that was, in a word that became ubiquitous, "mellow." The next day we barely had time for breakfast before beginning to dance to the raucous blues of Canned Heat followed by Big Brother and the Holding Company fronted by a new girl named Janis Joplin. Then we collapsed and listened while Country Joe and the Fish laid down their anti-war rock to roars of agreement. These festivities were easy to hear from outside the official concert area. You didn't need an extra ticket to enjoy yourself: The party was everywhere you looked. Hugh Masekela, the Byrds, Laura Nyro and Jefferson Airplane took us into the night until Otis Redding, with Booker T and the MGs tight behind him, worked us up with "Satisfaction" and finally settled us down by reminding us to "Try a Little Tenderness." Bliss.

Sunday morning Beth and I walked around, grazing from the food booths and soaking in the spirit. Here and there were uniformed policemen, but they had so little to do that they were smiling and accepting the blessings and flowers that were being offered to them by a crowd that reached over fifty thousand. People said there were three or four times that over the whole weekend. The assembly was racially mixed but largely white, though race was only one aspect of the diversity. There were older couples draped in turquoise and leather, bikers in jeans and vests, and girls in gauzy blouses clinging to bare breasts and perky nipples. Many fans looked like escapees from the corporate world: shorthaired guys and women with severely sprayed hairdos. The "squares" were looking to change their shape.

It was hard to imagine what could possibly top the previous day's experiences when a tall, affable "Johnny Acid Seed" came through the crowd handing out "tabs," slips of paper soaked with LSD. His offer was made casually and openly even though LSD had become illegal in California eight months earlier. He assured Beth and me that it was pure. We each absorbed one and took the trip. It seemed like the perfect time.

There was a small hill just outside the concert area that afforded a view onto the stage about two hundred feet away. We settled on a blanket there for the day's first entertainment, music we were assured we would find both unique and captivating. As the effect of this synthetic psychedelic took hold, Ravi Shankar began to pluck the strings of our minds with his sitar and Ali Raga drummed his tabla into our hearts over a steady drone. And there began an extrasensory journey of insights, colors, and visions that went on and on.

As a golden summer afternoon melted into evening, Beth and I drifted about in a magic bubble. After Buffalo Springfield played, we made our way back to the little hill and gazed down on the stage as the Who began rocking out. Pete Townshend said he was sending his music into space, bouncing it off satellites to England and back again: That was reverb. Maybe, maybe not, but I sensed an electric lasso encircling the globe connecting all of humanity. I felt completely, divinely linked to everyone and everything. Soon we were dancing to the Grateful Dead and sharing a joint with two Hells Angels who were ambling by. Then Jimi Hendrix strummed his greeting and carried on until he finally came to the end of "Wild Thing," set his guitar on fire, and smashed it to smithereens. It was crazy, scary, and raw, much like life outside our little haven. But it all fit.

I thought I was back on earth by the time the Mamas and the Papas offered up "California Dreaming" and bid us all a gentle and loving good night. We gathered up our tent and sleeping bags and sauntered out with thousands of new best friends. Unknowingly, we had kicked off what was soon labeled the "Summer of Love." Psychedelics and music insured that the Cultural Revolution did not begin with a "Fuck you!" It was set in motion with an "Oh, God!" a soft-core accompaniment to the hard-core battles over racism and the Vietnam War. Which isn't to say it always flowed so easily. Transitions were challenging, whether large scale or small.

Suddenly it fell to me as owner of the van to decide if we were *"going to San Francisco"* as Scott McKenzie had just sung or back to LA. I couldn't figure out what the criteria was for such a decision. I wasn't hallucinating, but I was still floating, not completely grounded. An unwelcome pressure began to build as we pulled into a gas station in Monterey. I tried to take care of business by checking the oil, and suddenly I couldn't even get the oil stick back into its long, slender tube. A tension gripped the back of my neck. It felt like a sinister homunculi or evil spirit had jumped me and was squeezing out the bliss, replacing it with doubt and fear.

I huddled in the back of my van in Beth's willing, but equally inexperienced, embrace. Mike hadn't trusted the free psychedelics, but he'd had some speed, and eagerly drove us back to LA. I was learning that there was no free trip in that exciting and perilous time. Psychedelics had a negative side: a shadow that often showed itself as paranoia. If you tripped out while your mind, to say nothing of your society, was in a state of flux, there might not be a safe harbor to return to. That complicated things for the upcoming Summer of Love and its budding culture.

7

NONVIOLENT VIOLENCE

Two months after the massive demonstrations in New York and San Francisco, Los Angeles had its first big anti-war protest. The idea was to embarrass President Johnson when he came to raise money in the Century City Plaza hotel for $1,000 a plate. The police expected one thousand anti-war protestors, maybe two. Fifteen thousand people showed up singing and carrying placards, all in the spirit of nonviolent protest. This largely middle-class demonstration had been revved up earlier in the day by speeches from both H. Rap Brown and Dr. Benjamin Spock and had their draft cards signed by the most famous draft resister, Muhammad Ali. It was cool until the crowd stopped to chant slogans in front of the hotel where LBJ was selling the war. When they didn't disperse, the cops freaked out, waded in with batons, and beat the crap out of them: whites, blacks, hippies, and professionals in suits.

I didn't go. I had some vague idea that the war might be running down and told myself I'd already done my part. But I talked some friends into going, including Jaimo, who hung out at the commune sometimes. It was all over the radio and local TV. Some of the reporters tried to blame the anti-war protestors, but you could tell it was just the kind of scene that Johnson was trying to avoid.

Jaimo showed up banging on my door that night with a bandaged head. "It was fucking insane, man! Nobody heard the order to disperse, and those chickenshit bastards rushed us and knocked over my grandmother. I got on top of her to protect her and they whacked me twice before moving on."

"You almost got your grandmother beat up?" I exclaimed.

"You thought you were the one who talked me into going, but she was the real reason. She wanted LBJ to know that white-haired old ladies also think this war stinks." He gingerly touched his bandage. "She's really pissed. She's already registered a complaint against the LAPD and called the ACLU."

"So the old lady is leading her hippie grandson astray," I cracked.

"Man, I just thank the White Rabbit that I wasn't tripping. That would have been a real bummer." He handed me a still camera I'd loaned him. "I didn't even take one picture before I got hit." He groaned, "I'm splittin' to San Fran for a while. This place is giving me a headache."

Jaimo wasn't alone that summer. "Peace and Love" echoed from the Be-Ins, Love-Ins, and other "tribal" gatherings, an enticing Siren's song to young people across the land. They rolled like loose marbles from all over the country to San Francisco for a "Summer of Love." "Dropping out" became a path to personal freedom and awareness. It was vaguely utopian, and many felt a religious impulse and considered the psychedelic drug use to be Eucharistic. It was also true that pure numbers overwhelmed that city, and soon it was crowded with as many lost souls as enlightened ones. One could condemn it or be awed by it: It depended upon where you looked. But you couldn't ignore that young people were in revolt against the culture of their parents. We were in a social upheaval that was both enticing and complicated. In its own way it was dangerous, but it wasn't nearly as dangerous as the simultaneous civil rights revolution.

The race riot that blazed in the summer of 1965 in Watts spread to more places in 1966 and scared the hell out of more people. The movement for racial equality that had upended the South for over a decade continued its move north with a vengeance that summer of '67. Alarmed and energized, many working-class whites reacted to "uppity blacks" just as Paul said they would. However, LBJ's Great Society had declared a "War on Poverty," and there were high hopes that America was, at last, on track to live up to the ideals of its founding fathers. Since 1964, this Texan had put millions of dollars into federal programs to tackle the underpinnings of inequality that had made the ghettos such scenes of desperation. But change, once promised, didn't come soon enough for some.

"Motherfucking motherfuckers" was how my dealer Stanley put it. It was July 26, 1967, and we were kicking back in my studio, enjoying a taste of the grass he was selling when we heard a news report that Federal troops had been sent to Detroit, where rioting was out of control. "Fucking pigs didn't shoot enough brothers in Newark?" he said almost to himself.

"Pigs," I echoed without thinking, using this provocative slur for the first time. Immediately I felt conflicted. I still had the .22 rifle that Chief Kettman of the Palm Springs Police Department had given me for my ninth birthday. He'd been a close family friend. He was no pig but he was a little intimidating and I was sure he'd be out there "upholding the law."

Stanley was talking about far angrier cops who had gone out of control in Newark two weeks earlier. There, the police and poorly trained National Guard reacted with far more deadly violence than the rioters, shooting without warning and killing randomly. Twenty-six were dead by the time it stopped.

"Motherfuckers think we're the goddamn Viet Cong or something," Stanley continued. I'd met him at school, where he worked in the Motion Picture department. Another student had directed me to him when I said I wanted to buy a still camera. He'd sold me a new Nikon for a suspiciously low price, but I figured it best not to question how he got his supply.

"Were you living in LA during the Watts riot?" I asked.

He said he'd been raised around USC in a black neighborhood that stretched southward, gradually shrugging off its tidy, working-class homes until it turned into the projects of the Watts ghetto. I asked about his parents and he answered that his dad had worked for the city, picking up garbage.

"It was a good job 'for a Negro,'" Stanley explained in a mocking tone. He looked around at all my paintings leaning against the wall. "Problem is, he really was an artist. He could draw better than he could talk. He made crazy sculptures out of the junk he picked up as he worked: a stuffed black bird escaping from the rake jaws of a white alligator. He had that shit all around the backyard except where my mom claimed space for her garden."

"Sounds like he'd get on well with the Dadaists. Did he ever sell anything?" I asked.

"Yeah, to friends. He tried some galleries but, you know, the owners didn't know how to promote it. After a while my dad began to doubt he was good enough."

The newsman announced that it was estimated that more than two thousand stores had been looted or burned but that the troops appeared to be stopping Detroit's slide into complete chaos. "I'm getting tired of bad news," I said and flipped the radio dial to the jazz station.

"You know that Detroit was the model city for these new Federal programs," Stanley said, "the ones where 'The Man' was going to make up for slavery and for sending all these black boys to Vietnam and to mark the end of poverty." He laughed disdainfully. "Nobody realized that they were going to model Detroit after fucking Saigon."

I nodded in agreement but I didn't know what to say. We sat, enjoying the buzz, listening to Miles on "So What." "What happened to your dad?" I asked. "You use the past tense when you talk about him."

"He's alive, sort of... Two years ago he took a stray bullet in the spine during the riots, or rebellion, as we say. He's paralyzed from the waist down, so working is in the past tense." Stanley paused then added, "He went out on the street to make sure there were no fires nearby and got hit...probably some brother blasting the shit out of something nearby since the bullet didn't match anything the police or guard were using."

"That's really messed up," I said, "getting shot by your own people."

Stanley looked at me with a flash of irritation. "He used to say, 'Everybody's my people,' but, then again, he believed in integration." He swallowed the roach. "Me, I say, 'Nobody's my people' and 'What's holding up the fucking revolution.'"

"Man, I'm sorry about your dad. Do you think he'd dig a book on Dada? I've got one I'd be happy to give to him."

"Why?" Stanley cocked his head, looking at me.

"It's not easy being an artist. You can use all the inspiration you can get."

Stanley allowed a shy smile. "Shit, why not. He could use a little inspiration." He sighed. "No different than the rest of us, I guess."

I got Robert Motherwell's *The Dada Painters and Poets* off a shelf. "I think he'll dig it. Hell, you might get something from those crazy fuckers."

Stanley looked skeptical, but took the book.

"I do think things are going to get better," I added.

"Why?"

"I guess because they have to."

Stanley laughed. "Hell, man, go ahead and be optimistic if it makes you feel good. Whatever helps, know what I mean?"

I nodded.

"You gonna buy the motherfuckin' dope," he asked, "or just make up happy thoughts on your own?"

I paid him ninety bucks for a kilo and he split. Some people living at the commune had asked me to score. They'd get most of the 2.2 pounds of dope at the price I paid. I kept a small stash. Some of them were probably selling it elsewhere, but I didn't care. It was a stupid law. People were smoking dope openly more and more. It wasn't that rare to smell it walking down the street, and it was all over the Love-Ins and Be-Ins. But it was still against the law.

Beth returned from a class, cleaned my stash, had a hit from a joint, and took a nap. She wasn't really turned on by school. She was sweet, bright, and a willing model, but she always seemed to be around. It was like she hadn't had a life before we met. Still, the sex was good and she didn't get in the way of my painting, so I figured there was nothing, really, to complain about.

A few weeks later, she and I drove over to the commune only to see cops coming out the door. I didn't trust how they'd react to some longhair questioning them, so I had Beth find out what was going on.

She came back to the car crying. "Busted! They took six people away about an hour ago. They said the door was open and they went upstairs to investigate a 'potential robbery' and found hippies smoking dope." She wailed, "It's so unfair."

It took until the next day but we finally found them at the jail downtown. Warren and Heidi were outside on the sidewalk as we rolled up. "Praise the Lord, we were just released," he said. He seemed quite calm, smoking his pipe, and rather philosophical about the whole mess. He explained that everyone was being held on $3,000 bail. To get out, each one had to post bond for that amount plus pay $300 upfront to the bail bondsman.

"It's been an interesting twenty-four hours," he said. "I only had resources to post bond for the two of us. Wolf and Edie are going to wait for the hearing because they're sure the charges will be dropped."

Heidi broke in, "Those idiots didn't have a warrant, so they'll never make it stick. Even so, Angie wants out, but she can't tell her parents and doesn't have any money. She promised she would pay the $300 back soon."

"That leaves Rondo," Warren said. "He's the one I'm worried about. He's flippin' out in there."

"Where's his father?" I asked.

Warren cocked his eyebrow. "I don't know where he lives, but Rondo said his dad would never bail him out. He also insisted that he'd go crazy if he had to spend any more time behind bars. I don't think he was exaggerating."

Heidi looked intently at me and finally said, "Come on, Dennis. It's time to put some of your daddy's money where your heart is."

Warren and Heidi knew I wasn't working or making money on my art other than a few prints I'd sold at a student exhibition. They also knew that I lived off a trust. My heart was pounding. I wasn't comfortable having money. It made me feel like a phony, like I couldn't count on myself to survive. But it's not that I wanted to give it away so much as I wanted others to have enough too. Now I was being asked to stand behind the advantage I had.

"How much?" I asked, even though I'd just heard the figures.

"You put up $300 per person, along with proof you can cover the full $3,000 if that person jumps bail," Warren said.

When it came down to it, it didn't seem like I had any choice, so I bailed Rondo and Angie out of jail and went back to my art. Two weeks later, the day of the hearing, I decided to shoot a few rolls of black-and-white film with my new camera around the neighborhood and ended up at the commune.

I could hear people excitedly chattering as I came up the stairs and learned that the charges had been dropped as predicted. Warren came over through the dim light and handed me a glass of wine. "Our prayers were answered. It's all cool…except Rondo split. He didn't show up for the hearing as ordered. Now there's a warrant out for his arrest."

"What the hell does that mean?"

"It means he jumped bail, and you're on the hook for the whole $3,000," Warren answered.

"Fuck no," I groaned. "Is that why they got a warrant out for him?"

"To get you your money back?" Warren laughed. "No, I'm afraid they want to put him back in jail for breaking the conditions of his parole."

"Parole?" I shouted.

"Turns out that's why he was so anxious to get out. He's been in jail since he was sixteen. He figured it was just a matter of time before they found his records, and he'd be back in jail just for getting arrested."

"Does anyone know where Franklin lives, or did he run away too?" I barked in disgust.

From a couch in the shadows, Franklin's gravelly baritone rumbled over. "Not like me to run."

I walked over to him and Mavis seated on the couch. I'd heard that they'd coupled up. "Well, this is fucked up, isn't it?" I said, trying to sound even-tempered.

"It looks like the boy did what he had to do. He's paying for his mistakes just like the rest of us."

"Unless he's planning to get me $3,000, it doesn't sound like he's paying for anything, unless you're going to cover it and put it on his bill."

"Not me, pal. I got hip to his shit a long time ago, and he knows what I'll do and won't do. He's his own man."

I stared at him, trembling with frustration. "That seems like a chickenshit way out of being a father."

"Not at all," Franklin said calmly. "You, him, me," he gestured to the people scattered around the loft who were listening to us, "everyone here takes their chances, makes their choices, and then has to live with them." He sighed. "Now, admittedly, some are a little poorer in the pocket, but we're all richer from the experience."

"Fuck you, Franklin," I said. "It's easy for you to say since you didn't take any risks."

"Don't lose sight of your values, my friend, just because they cost you something," he responded evenly. "What you did was generous and thoughtful, if a bit foolhardy."

"Like I said, fuck you!"

"Would you have tried to talk one of the others here out of making Rondo's bail if they had been able to cover it?" I was silent and he continued, "No, because it was the right thing for one of you to do. But I could give you eighteen years of reasons why it wasn't right for me." His voice followed me as I began to walk away, pissed and disgusted. "And isn't $3,000 worth the freedom of a young man?"

Angie came over and gave me a big hug. "Thank you again, Dennis. I sorry you got burned by Rondo, but you really saved me." I hugged her back and she put some bills in my hand. "Here's fifty. I should be able to pay you that much from my tips every two weeks."

Several others gathered around and thanked me for being there for Rondo and Angie, and for "not letting 'The Man' bring us down."

Wolf, with his beard halfway down his chest, and his partner Edie were the ones who'd spent the two weeks in jail. They both looked worn out, but Wolf seemed relieved. "We're going to split to the Sierras and get the fuck out of civilization for a while. We'll probably end up in a commune near Petaluma, but now we need to leave the bad vibes behind."

"It's the pigs' own fault," Edie claimed angrily. "If they'd leave us alone, we could peacefully change the society—but when they push us like this, they only bring on the revolution faster."

"Edie doesn't mind if it gets more violent," Wolf said. "But that's not my bag. I'm like, 'turn the other cheek,' you know?"

Angie said, "Come on, Dennis. We're going to see this far-out film, *The Battle of Algiers*. It's about the liberation movement against France."

"It's the end of fucking colonialism!" Edie enthused. "It's happening all around the world."

I declined. I'd just blown $3,000 on somebody I barely knew and would probably never see again. That was enough to live on for an entire year, and my trust wasn't going to last forever. I felt much more like a sucker than a hero. I hurried down the stairs to the street. "Goddamn it!" I repeated until I felt a surge of the old Catholic guilt over using His name in vain. "Fuck me," I muttered, feeling trapped every which way. I wandered through Lafayette Park and around the streets for over an hour. I remembered what I'd said to Stanley about being optimistic. Why was that, and what did that imply?

A lot of people were impatient and losing hope. Anger threatened to change the very nature of the civil rights movement. Dr. King's nonviolence and dream of equality were built on the idea of black assimilation into the general society. But, more and more, the call for integration was being replaced by demands for a whole new kind of society. Rebellion was edging toward revolution. Many younger blacks and the most leftist of SDS and the anti-war movement argued that America was too racist and imperialistic for voluntary change. They watched as wars of liberation broke out around the world and heard Che Guevara's call for "two, three, many Vietnams." More and more concluded, "Fuck it! Revolution now!"

But what the hell did that mean? Sara's friend Jerry hadn't made a convincing pitch for Marxism, and besides, before we got a new system, we'd have to win some kind of civil war. It looked to me that on one side there were the cops and the National Guard and, if necessary, the Army, but other than a few crazed individuals, not many were fighting back with guns. It meant that a lot of defenseless citizens were getting killed. Most recently, forty-three had ended up dying in Detroit.

I might be calling police "pigs," but I knew radical ideas were easier to shout than act on. Emotions could spark a riot, but a revolution took sustained, organized action, and that seemed impossible—not that there weren't hints of it. Some black guys in Oakland called the Black Panthers had started carrying guns the previous fall. But they weren't shooting them; they were clever and sophisticated. They believed in the U.S. Constitution so much that they would read from it aloud as they stood watching a policeman who'd pulled over one of their black brothers in the neighborhood. California law said it was their right to carry a gun, and once they stepped outside their cars, they could put a shell in the chamber of their twelve-gauge shotguns: *ka-chunk*. They were all-American. They scared the shit out of some and thrilled others, but they were essentially patriotic, participating citizens. They were upping the ante in the civil rights game, but they weren't necessarily revolutionaries. These cats may have been braver and more audacious than most, but at this point I figured they were part of the "New Left," since they were stressing nonviolence, even though it was in a most militant way.

There were a lot of ways to drop out: You could refuse to participate and get stoned; get away and create your own little world; or rebel against the system. Rebelling against the culture was one thing, but rebelling against the system was a whole other step.

I made my way to MacArthur Park and plopped down on a bench next to the little lake. When I was almost drafted, I became strongly anti-war, unless another Hitler came along. Since then I'd certainly become more of a rebel, but this wasn't the time for revolution. The laws were on our side, moving us toward greater justice. We didn't need to create a whole new system. We had a good one. What we needed was to keep pushing without losing our cool.

I took my camera and began looking around. However things turned out, life was moving very fast, and taking pictures seemed to slow it down. I took all kinds of shots: kids laughing like crazy as their paddleboat went in circles on the lake; ducks diving among the reeds; garbage in the palm trees; winos arguing with ghosts. It helped, but I needed to slow things down even further, and there was no better place than the desert.

At a pay phone, I called Beth and told her what had happened. I'd be back late. She complained that I wasn't paying enough attention to her. I didn't know what to say except "Sorry" and "See you later." I picked up some burritos and walked over to the house that Mike shared with some others. He and I ate, drank beer, developed the film, and printed a few photos. I invited him to go out to the desert the next day.

I woke up early the next morning. Beth slept at my side. I lay in bed thinking, feeling anxious to get away. Finally, I realized it was more specific than that. Beth stirred and went to the bathroom. When she returned, without really planning to, I told her I felt smothered and needed to live alone. She fell apart and we began to argue. After an hour, I couldn't stand it and told her I needed to take this outside.

We drove to Lafayette Park, but things only got worse. She began to sob and shriek, "I can't live without you." She kept pleading her dependence until something clicked in me. I stopped feeling guilty.

I looked gently at the fear in her eyes and insisted, "It's not true. You're strong, but you've been leaning on me way too much. It's made you think you're weak. But it's not true."

She stopped pleading. We talked a while longer until she was calm. I didn't tell her that I refused to be emotionally blackmailed and that her passive, helpless stuff was a turn-off. I didn't have to: She got it. She admitted that my change of heart wasn't a complete surprise and agreed to be gone when I returned in a few days.

8

FATHER AND SON

In 1914, my dad's parents homesteaded a wind-tormented 160 acres of burning sand and skittering chuckwallas outside of Palm Springs, California. This was about the most uninviting piece of land you could imagine: seasonal water at best, no trees, fiendish sandstorms, and 120 degrees in the summer. Grandfather Alvah was a journeyman carpenter, and Tess, my grandmother, was armed with a strict Roman Catholicism to help her keep the faith that living on the outskirts of hell was sure to test. But it was free—all yours if you built a dwelling, tried to grow something, and stayed for three years. It represented what remained at the end of the Homesteading era in America: free land that the government said was there for the taking. That's what drove Europeans to America and their kin out of the East Coast. These folks, ancestors of serfs, knew in their guts that a man's home was his castle, and, however poor, that made them kings and queens.

My dad was five and my uncle Milt was three when the train dropped the family off. Alvah quickly hammered together a small wooden cabin, slightly raised so the rattlers couldn't get in too easily. School was five miles away and fresh water was even farther, unless the streams were flowing. The kids traveled on a burro, often riding backward just to liven things up. Fortunately, Alvah was a hell of a carpenter, and after three years they moved into a home he designed and constructed in the sheltered oasis called Palm Springs. He sold it, created more, and pretty soon they didn't have to move again. One satisfied wealthy customer lent Grandpa Alvah enough money to buy the water company for this little village. It was just water running in ditches at the time. Soon, besides building homes, he began sinking wells and laying pipe to carry water from the surrounding canyons. Within ten years, he was a civic leader in that enchanting oasis as it slowly spread into the surrounding desert.

My dad grew up with the local Indian, white, and Mexican kids. He told stories of racing horses through the dry washes, skirting the cactus and creosote bushes, and watching the old Indian men play gambling games on the earthen floor of their huts. The village rested at the base of Mt. San Jacinto, a massive mountain, 10,834 feet high, which isolated them from Los Angeles, an emerging metropolis a hundred miles to the west. Tourists came for the beautiful weather and the healing hot springs. The town grew and Dad began to sell homes to the newcomers from his real estate office: "Palm Springs for Climate, Harold Hicks for Real Estate," the ads said.

Both Alvah and Tess died around the time I was born, and Dad became president of the water company. He carefully expanded it to meet the needs of our booming town. His success created the money that, thirty years later, would bail out my friends. But throughout my childhood, Dad was frugal and never lost sight of his hardscrabble early years. He was always quick to remind us kids that having money didn't mean you were better than someone without it. However, it did mean that we didn't have to worry about it. Growing up, I never thought of us as rich: We simply had enough. To my buddies and me, the rich were the tourists and movie stars who flocked to Palm Springs during the winter.

It was an amazingly carefree life until my mother went off to reclaim herself in Los Angeles. Not only did she leave my father and me to a bachelor life, she shattered the family beyond recognition. As I mentioned, my two oldest siblings were already in college, so they were only occasionally around. But she took Jeanie, the next oldest, with her. I never knew it until decades later, but Dad had bargained with my mom; he wouldn't contest the divorce, but she had to leave me, young Denny, with him. Dad didn't want to be alone. What I did know was that sadness seemed to ooze from the adobe brick walls of our family home. I cried every night, and my dad was in an emotional free fall for at least two years.

At the encouragement of Uncle Milt, his high-living brother, Dad began to date and catch up on all that he'd missed as an innocent Catholic virgin twenty years earlier, when he'd married. This was happening outside of my awareness until, while borrowing socks from his drawer, I came across condoms. My discovery made me furious. I loved my dad, but the rules that applied to my sex life and me applied to him as well. The Church was unequivocal: The only woman he was allowed to have sex with was his wife. It wasn't my fault if she wasn't around. How could he expect me to follow the rules if he didn't? It made no difference that I was fifteen and he was fifty-six. Rules were fucking rules. I was confident that this wasn't some childish tantrum: This was grown-up stuff. But, as righteous as I was about my dad's hypocrisy, it soon dawned on me that just because he was willing to risk going to Hell, I still had to answer to the priests myself, and I was sure they wouldn't let me off the hook simply because my dad was a sinner.

It got stranger. It wasn't long before Dad fell in love and married Mary Lindgren, a lovely Episcopalian. This meant that the Catholic Church officially excommunicated him. They didn't care who had divorced whom; it had been a legal marriage, so he wasn't allowed to marry again. To them, he was an unrepentant bigamist and was kicked off a team that I was still a member of. I was left holding onto the hope of making it into Heaven. No matter that I masturbated like an unhinged chimpanzee and felt under girls' sweaters like a lost, fevered explorer. As long as I confessed my sins, I had a chance at eternal salvation.

Other paradoxes unfolded from my father's post-divorce journey. He decided he needed to get healthier and, at the advice of a doctor friend, gave up alcohol and cigarettes. He'd been a pretty heavy drinker and smoker, and quitting definitely made him more present. He began to go through various spiritual and psychological changes. By the time I took my first drug trip in Columbus in 1966, he was going to seminars on Buddhism and Gestalt therapy at the Esalen Institute in Big Sur. He even tried mescaline. He began meditating and hanging out with various gurus, sages, and teachers. My father, the businessman, became a spiritual seeker, his own version of a hippie. He didn't exactly drop out; he wandered about. He didn't make a big deal out of rejecting society. It was more like he was set free and went his own way, looking for a deeper meaning to his life.

Although we never explicitly acknowledged this, my father and I evolved and matured with the Cultural Revolution at the same time and for similar reasons. We were both escaping the effects of strict Roman Catholicism. We were both reclaiming our sexuality and opening ourselves to new experiences. In effect, we were both drawn to living in the moment. It was particularly challenging because, though we hadn't thought of it this way until we each ran into meditation and Buddhist philosophy, Catholics are trained not to live in the moment. Instead, we were taught to deny all sorts of things in the present in order to get a better future. The saving grace for each of us may have been that, from our earliest years, we'd been deeply influenced by the vast and absorbing desert, where the present moment seemed to stretch out forever.

In the late 1940s, Dad had bought a cabin about twenty minutes from Palm Springs. It was hidden away in a canyon on a different face of Mt. San Jacinto, and its creek supplied some of the water for the town. The cabin had no telephone or electricity and for years it was where he retreated for solace. Eventually it became my refuge whenever I returned home and didn't want to stay with either him or my mom in Palm Springs. A triangle of immense white granite boulders fanned across the mouth of the canyon like a rocky apron. No matter how much the world's problems plagued me, if I could scramble through that boulder field and ascend the rushing stream into the mountain's embrace, relief was there.

I worried about Dad's reaction to my losing $3,000 and asked him to meet me at the cabin. He came up the second day. I made plans with Mike to join us later, and Dad and I went for a walk. First I told him I'd broken up with my girlfriend. He didn't have much to say except he didn't think he was the best one to give relationship advice. I was cool with that. Besides, I knew we wouldn't always agree. He certainly didn't view politics as I did. But he wasn't too judgmental. He was a pragmatic sort of Republican, big on individual responsibility sprinkled with compassion.

We were sitting with our feet in the icy stream when I finally told the story about losing the money. Trees shaded us from the broiling summer sun that had pushed the temperature to what felt like a hundred degrees. He was silent for a long time. Pursed lips indicated he was upset, or at least concerned, but he said nothing until he gave out a big sigh and said, "I started trusts for everyone's education, long before your mom got the divorce. Part of our agreement was that I'd cover your education, and you each would get what was left over when you were twenty-one. In return for taking care of your education, she agreed not to take so much alimony that I would have to sell the Water Company."

"Sell it! Why?"

"Community property...she was due half of whatever I had made while we were married...she was more than fair. It could have cost me a lot more...financially." The swish of the stream muted the sad undertone of his thoughts. His green eyes glinted at me in the dappled sunshine. "The question is, will losing that $3,000 change anything for you?"

My mind was reeling; I'd had no idea of my parents' negotiations, but I tried to answer his question. "Well, at first I was pissed off and felt like a fool. I still feel a little guilty...but proud, too. Mostly, I don't know what to feel, but that's not new." I hesitated. "As for losing the money, it's okay for now. Eventually, things will depend on whether people buy my paintings."

"Over the years, I've come to know many men far, far wealthier than me. As I've said to you often, watching them proved that money alone won't make you happy. Money is power. It can be used in many ways." He threw a stick into the rippling stream, and we watched it disappear over a short falls. "No one likes to feel like a fool. But it sounds like you may have given someone a chance at straightening out his life. Sometimes that's the greatest gift of all, having someone do something for you that shakes you out of your old ways."

I don't know why but I asked, "Dad, do you still believe in Heaven?"

"Some part of me still does." He chuckled. "You can kick the man out of the Church easier than you can kick the Church out of the man."

I began to disagree but he continued. "Six months ago I went to a workshop given by Alan Watts up at Esalen. Smart guy: able to explain Buddhism, meditation, and the spiritual life in impressively clear terms. We became quite friendly over the weekend, and I invited him down to the house. He visited last weekend and it turns out that, in addition to being somewhat enlightened, he's also an alcoholic."

I began to launch into something about hypocrisy, but he continued in a serious tone. "It seems that everyone wants enlightenment or Heaven or happiness or whatever, but if we want something too badly, we usually end up further away from it."

"Is that what happened to you and Mom?" The question just popped out.

He appeared surprised but answered, "That was part of it. I was too gung-ho on being a success and not focused enough on my marriage." He put his hand in the stream and splashed the back of his neck.

Whether for him or for me, I felt embarrassed. We hadn't ever really talked about the reasons for the divorce. There were many things I could have asked, but the moment evaporated as Mike appeared on the ridge and lumbered down to the river with tuna sandwiches. We ate after we went skinny dipping in the bracing water.

At some point Dad asked me if I believed in Heaven.

"Not anymore." I shook my head. "I think we're here to expand our consciousness, and improve the world even if that turns out to be impossible."

Dad smiled. "I would agree, but so would Ronald Reagan—as least when he was spokesman for General Electric. He said, 'Progress is our most important product.'"

I laughed. "I guess Reagan and I have to agree on something."

"But it's tricky. Alan spoke of a Chinese curse: 'May you live in interesting times.'"

"They're interesting, that's for damn sure," Mike said. "But are you optimistic?"

"I'm not much for predictions." Dad paused. "But I'm excited and curious. That's a lot like optimism."

Driving back to LA a day later, Mike said, "Your dad's cool."

I passed the joint back to him and asked why.

"Well, skinny dipping dads are pretty rare," he joked.

"Skinny Dipping Dads: sounds like a rock group." I exhaled.

"Seriously, man, he's pretty thoughtful about our place in this fucked-up world. I don't even mind that he seems optimistic, 'cause I think he sees the bad stuff, unlike you."

"I see the bad stuff, asshole. The difference between you and me is that you don't trust that the people can change this government. But that's what our democracy is all about, having a system where the people change what's screwed up. We're moving from passive to active resistance."

Mike laughed at my earnestness and turned up the volume on the Doors' "The End." He was an anarchist at heart, and he was quite content with things falling apart. Our argument went on and continued as the fall of 1967 unfolded. It was getting more and more disconcerting to be standing up for this country, but I couldn't believe it could stay this bad forever.

One thing we could agree on was that TV, the newspapers, and magazines tried to co-opt everything and use it to sell something. The so-called hippie phenomenon was being completely poisoned.

Less than six months after the first Be-In, *Time, Look, Saturday Evening Post,* and other magazines slobbered all over the counterculture, trying to wrap it up, define, and limit it. So we killed the hippie. "We" in this case was a group in San Francisco called the Diggers, a particularly brilliant and socially minded band of rebellious souls. They did street theater that pushed change in people's faces: They drove a truck of semi-naked belly dancers through San Francisco's financial district, enticing brokers and bankers out of their offices to jump on board and leave their soul-sucking work behind. To celebrate "The Death of Hippie" in October, they staged a parade through the Haight-Ashbury, the countercultural center of the world. Masked citizens carried a coffin with the words "Hippie—Son of Media" on the side. Mike and I were jazzed to see this invention of the media be so labeled, and delighted to know that the media coverage would take the message to millions.

At the same time, Mike insisted, "We haven't changed shit. Under this system anything really radical will be co-opted by Madison Avenue, if not destroyed by outright violence. Corporate capitalism is in control, and we'll be fighting wars and wasting money until we change it."

As if to prove his point, the CIA in Bolivia tracked down and assassinated Che Guevara. His death photo was shown around the world, should anyone doubt that the USA would go anywhere to stop liberation movements.

More and more people insisted that the reaction to liberation movements was happening right here. At the end of October, Huey Newton, the co-founder of the Black Panther Party for Self-Defense, was shot and arrested for killing a police officer in Oakland, CA. Countless demonstrations challenged his guilt, and the Black Panthers took up the call. "Free Huey! Off the pig!" Circumstances were pushing these black men, and others, from the realm of protest into resistance. The specter of revolution was hovering in the wings.

Every time something outrageous happened, Mike would do an impression of the crocodile in *Peter Pan.* "Tick tock, tick tock, the country is about to explode." He had no shortage of reasons. There were close to half a million American soldiers in Vietnam. Almost every night on TV, you could see coffins wrapped in American flags returning. Tens of thousands marched to the Pentagon and, led by Allen Ginsberg, attempted to "levitate" it.

"So much for meditating our way out of this mess," Mike observed.

But there was another way of looking at things, and some part of me stayed hopeful: Thurgood Marshall was confirmed as the first black American Justice of the Supreme Court, and another black man, Carl Stokes, was elected mayor of Cleveland. In mid-November, President Johnson reported to the American people about Vietnam, "We are inflicting greater losses than we're taking... We are making progress." A few days later, General Westmoreland boasted to news reporters, "I am absolutely certain that whereas in 1965 the enemy was winning, today he is certainly losing." Then he scuttled back to Vietnam, where he insisted that the enemy was losing soldiers at a rate of ten for every one of ours. Whether we were winning or losing, the demands to end the war steadily increased, and that was cause for hope. The anti-war movement and SDS were more active than ever. While some Marxist/Leninist parties raised the call for violent revolution, most of the energy and people came from the nonviolent New Left. Many of them swarmed around Senator Eugene McCarthy, who had announced his candidacy for the Democratic Party presidential nomination challenging LBJ. One could be an anti-war radical and enthusiastically support the electoral process. There were even hints that Bobby Kennedy would join the race, and he was a guy who could beat LBJ and whatever Republican war hawk was nominated. This all pointed to being patient and working within the system. I wanted to believe it, but I didn't want to fall victim to blind faith like I had as a child to Catholic dogma. After Christmas, I returned to Dad's cabin for a few days by myself to hike and meditate.

I had a cautious relationship with meditating. I knew that sitting quietly and calming myself was a potent tool. Some people likened it to prayer. I knew about that. Even before I took my first communion,

I'd gone to my knees and recited my prayers every night. And following their divorce, I'd prayed to God for years to bring my parents back together. Somewhere in my teens, I stopped.

In the time since I came back from New York, I experimented with different meditations that were being taught by a wide variety of gurus and teachers who populated the spiritual landscape. I received and used a mantra from Maharishi's Transcendental Meditation, whom the Beatles had made famous. I had a brief fling with an enthralling woman that included several sessions of chanting *Nam-myoho-renge-kyo* with her Nichiren Buddhism group. I was initiated into Subud, a quirky, quasi-secret society, and practiced yoga as taught by Satchidananda. I even learned an intriguing meditation technique from Roy Masters, a conservative talk-radio host. I found that each one offered something of value that had a powerful yet subtle influence on me as well as on the broader culture.

However, my experience with psychotherapy had forced me to acknowledge that I was very good at denying and repressing any negative feelings I had. And most meditations seemed to be easily subverted into techniques for emotional repression, like handing problems off to a higher power. I knew I didn't need any help in that area. However, it reflects the depth and variation of the spiritual ferment of the times that there was also a voice for this caution in J. Krishnamurti, a sort of anti-guru. Since the 1920s when he was a young man, he had successfully resisted the role of "enlightened teacher" that was thrust upon him over and over. He wrote and taught continuously, disabusing his fans of making him into something they might have thought they needed but which he knew he wasn't.

Krishnamurti spent a lot of time in Ojai, just over an hour from Los Angeles, where I attended a few of his talks. What influenced me the most was when he said: "Meditation is the most extraordinary thing if you know how to do it, and you cannot possibly learn from anybody: That's the beauty of it. It isn't something you learn, a technique, and therefore there is no authority. Learn about yourself, watch yourself, watch the way you walk, the way you talk, how you eat, what you say, the gossip, the hate, the jealousy. If you are aware of it... all that is part of meditation. Meditation is not following a system; it is not repetition, a constant imitation. Meditation is something that demands an astonishingly alert mind, great sensitivity in which there is no sense of bringing something about through demand because... that experience obviously will be according to your conditioning."

His teaching was challenging, similar to pondering the Zen koan, "What is the sound of one hand clapping?" However, it was also personally empowering. Trusting myself and finding authority within was very attractive, since I had fought so hard to free myself from the fundamentalist dogma and control of the Catholic Church.

The second day at the cabin, I decided to meditate in the classic way: sitting on a pillow. I was straight, not stoned. I focused on my breathing, and my mind quieted. For what seemed like several minutes, I seemed to float with only momentary thoughts, images, or emotions passing through. Then, a tight squeezing began at the back of my neck, as if a malevolent force or spirit had slipped in. I recognized it. This was the same paranoia that had gripped me at the end of my LSD trip after the Monterey Pop Festival. It had occasionally reappeared when I smoked grass, something I did every few days. But this was the first time it had appeared in full force when I wasn't stoned. It was painful but free-floating, not connected to any thought or cause. It was pure anxiety, an uptight, throbbing, debilitating tension just for its own sake. But I was so calm when it showed up that I was able to observe my fear, intimidation, and physical discomfort, and not be overwhelmed. I sat with the pain and breathed into it. Nothing seemed to change. After a while, I turned my attention around as though to look at this intruder gripping my neck. I indicated that I was no longer willing to coexist with it. I told it that if it wanted to continue with me, it needed to do more, take further control or leave. I sensed I was taking a great risk. Immediately it squeezed my neck even more painfully, two, three times. I held on, submitting to it but repeating my demand: *Do more, or go.* After one final wrenching constriction, it released its grip and disappeared out the same window of my mind that it had come in. It seemed like an auspicious way to begin the new year, 1968.

9

THE WAR COMES HOME

As 1967 ended, General Westmoreland was called back from Vietnam to Washington, D.C., to confront doubts and flagging enthusiasm for the war he was leading. He proudly announced, "We have reached an important point, when the end begins to come into view," and said that we could see "the light at the end of the tunnel." He also damned the anti-war demonstrators as "unpatriotic." Less than six weeks later, on January 30, 1968, "the light at the end of the tunnel" turned out to be the flames from the explosions from a linked series of surprise attacks by North Vietnamese and Viet Cong that lit up over one hundred towns and cities across South Vietnam. It went on for weeks. They were strong, audacious, and they were everywhere: the Tet Offensive.

Even before the smoke cleared, the Administration claimed that the North Vietnamese had shot their wad in this effort and would be unable to continue militarily if only we hung in there. It was a feeble defense. The Tet Offensive was a singular disaster for the hawks in control of American foreign policy. Overnight the support for the war went from 60% to 42%. In some part of the national psyche, the war was lost, a realization that I sensed would never change. I wasn't the only one who was losing faith in my government.

Like the child in "The Emperor's New Clothes," the anti-war demonstrators had pointed out to the rest of the citizens what they couldn't or wouldn't acknowledge: The general and his military, and the President and his administration, were naked, bare-assed liars. It confirmed to millions that the United States government, having lied about how strong their opponent was and who was winning the war, was not to be trusted about anything. It made me wonder if the system was worth saving. I, Republican born and bred, was having radical thoughts, maybe even revolutionary ones. It was exciting. It was scary. And the risk was still personal. After all, that Army shrink had classified me as *1-Y*. That meant I "qualified only in case of war or national emergency." Technically Congress had passed a "joint resolution" to send troops to Vietnam, not a formal "declaration of war." But would that distinction exempt me as more and more Americans died?

The fighting during Tet was particularly furious. In one instance, allied commanders bombed and shelled a Vietnamese provincial capital, Ben Tre, without regard for civilian casualties in order to rout the Viet Cong. The Associated Press famously quoted an American major, "It became necessary to destroy the town to save it." That week alone in mid-February, 1968 saw 543 Americans killed in action and 2,547 wounded, the highest weekly toll of our soldiers to date.

Demands for peace negotiations erupted in disparate elements of American society, but one surprised me and gave me a glimmer of hope. With a few exceptions, my generation considered the corporate "establishment" to be bought off. Over and over, anti-war protestors pointed out that those who were deeply invested in the status quo controlled the news. So it was heartening and shocking when the grandfatherly dean of American newsmen, Walter Cronkite, returned from a visit to Vietnam to assess the aftermath of the Tet Offensive and forcefully blasted American officials for misleading the public and misrepresenting the progress of the war. Broadcasting on February 27, he said, "It seems now more certain than ever that the bloody experience of Vietnam is to end in a stalemate." He warned against further escalation, which he reminded us might include mutual use of nuclear weapons, for "…with each escalation, the world comes closer to the brink of cosmic disaster." He then stepped out of the historical role of the American journalist, that of neutral observer and advised negotiation: "...not as victors, but as an honorable people who lived up to their pledge to defend democracy, and did the best they could."

Two weeks later, Gene McCarthy came within 230 votes of beating LBJ in the New Hampshire Democratic primary. In contrast, Richard Nixon, who'd lost to John F. Kennedy for the presidency in 1960, as well as a bid to be governor in California in 1962, returned from the political graveyard and won for the Republicans, all the while insisting that America needed more "law and order." A few days later Robert F. Kennedy joined the presidential race. There were howls that he was opportunistic and ruthless, but his journey in the years since the anguish of his brother's assassination had given him a soulfulness to go along with his undeniable magnetism. Whether you were radical or conservative, stoned or frothing at the mouth about something that was wrong, you had to admit that things were getting interesting.

In the middle of this ferment, the American government, in the form of the Kerner Commission created by LBJ to investigate the causes of the race riots the summer before, made a rare if not unique public admission: "Our nation is moving toward two societies, one black, one white—separate and unequal." They strongly insisted that the riots occurred because of the frustration of urban blacks over their lack of economic opportunity and "white racism." Conservatives complained that the report took the rioters off the hook, and that if economics and racism were the causes, why hadn't the even poorer and more racist regions of the South exploded in flames? LBJ appeared to ignore the political hand grenade handed him by the Commission, but on March 31, 1968, we found out that on some level even the President was overwhelmed by the situation.

Mike and I were in Sears shopping for a jigsaw for one of my painting projects when, far across the room, we spied LBJ's face looming on six TV screens at once. We couldn't hear what he was saying, but his sad eyes spoke of many tortured hours spent considering whatever was on his mind. He looked like a beaten hound dog pleading for understanding. It was almost enough to make you feel sorry for the guy—almost. We raced closer to hear the President. Only three years earlier, he'd been elected by the largest margin in history. Yet, as we got within earshot, we heard him announce he wouldn't run for reelection. We were floored. He went on to say he didn't want to sacrifice the gains of the last few years by involving the presidency in the "partisan divisions" that roiled the country.

This was one crazy Texan. He had pushed through the most progressive civil rights changes since Lincoln—which half the country was apoplectic about—and he had expanded an imperialistic intervention into a conflagration that the other half of America passionately opposed. LBJ was half social radical and half reactionary warmonger. He'd shuffled the two together and pissed off nearly everyone. Now he said he wanted to negotiate an "honorable peace" and could only do so if he was no longer a player in partisan politics. One could only hope. I agreed that he could still save his legacy if he could end this war, even if he didn't seem to have an answer for the expanding civil crisis.

We jumped around cheering with a few other shoppers, but the exhilaration soon gave way to a chill as we tried to anticipate what it meant when the captain jumped ship. I wanted to believe that our nation would be able to transform the country peacefully. Given his thoughtful criticism of the war, Dr. King seemed like a reasonable choice for someone who could take us through rough times: a moderate, Christian black man with anti-war credentials. His doctrine of nonviolence had been dramatically tested, but it represented our better selves and our best chance. He didn't have to be President: That was too far out considering our racist history. But he was definitely the soul of a future that could work for all Americans.

It was not to be. Four days later on Thursday, April 4th, while he was in Memphis, Tennessee, to march for equal pay for the city's black garbage men, Martin Luther King, Jr. was assassinated. Unlike innumerable acts of racial hatred in the past, this violent, racist attack was met with a tidal wave of anguish and rage. It was as if the whole country shattered into black and white pieces. In the following days and weeks, 110 inner-cities exploded in riots and 46 people died, more civil unrest and violence than in the previous three years combined.

But not all cities came apart. The very evening that Dr. King was shot, Bobby Kennedy, campaigning for the Democratic nomination for President for less than three weeks, landed in Indianapolis, Indiana, to speak to a largely black inner-city audience. The police chief warned Kennedy that he could not assure protection and that giving a speech would be too dangerous. He chose to speak anyway. Some in the audience may have known that King had been shot, but few could have known he was dead. Kennedy himself had just learned it as he came off the plane. After shocking his listeners with the news of the death of Dr. King, here is what Bobby said:

"For those of you who are black and are tempted to…be filled with hatred and mistrust of the injustice of such an act, against all white people, I would only say that I can also feel in my own heart the same kind of feeling. I had a member of my family killed, but he was killed by a white man."

Few white men in our nation had the stature to step past the rigid confines of race and racism and invite that compassionate comparison. It was the first time he had spoken publicly of the assassination of his brother. Bobby spoke less than five minutes, making it up as he went along. He quoted from Aeschylus, his favorite poet: "Even in our sleep, pain which cannot forget falls drop by drop upon the heart, until, in our own despair, against our will, comes wisdom through the grace of God."

In spite of our outrage and sharp-edged grief, he said we needed love, wisdom, and compassion, not hatred, violence, and lawlessness. And he ended by asking that we "dedicate ourselves to what the Greeks wrote so many years ago: to tame the savageness of man and make gentle the life of this world." There were no riots in Indianapolis.

Bobby Kennedy dared to join with black America in their anger and loss and, even as the wound was most fresh, to lay the ground for national healing. He was the voice for trust in the system. The next day, Stokely Carmichael, who had left SNCC and joined the Black Panther Party, spoke from the streets of Washington, D.C. While he cautioned against mob violence, he made the case for revolution: "White America killed Dr. King last night. She made [it] a whole lot easier for a whole lot of black people today. There no longer needs to be intellectual discussions; black people know that they have to get guns. White America will live to cry that she killed Dr. King last night. It would have been better if she had killed Rap Brown and/or Stokely Carmichael, but when she killed Dr. King, she lost." Poor and even middle-class blacks, especially in Washington, D.C., Baltimore, and Chicago, nearly destroyed their own communities in their fury as white citizens armed in preparation for the presumed race war that was on the horizon.

I drove to the desert to get some paintings I'd left at my mom's house. Paul was stuck in front of the television, oddly quiet and non-communicative. Mom was in the kitchen making herself her favorite lunch: a liverwurst, Swiss cheese sandwich with a glass of buttermilk. I'd watched her eat this combo for many years before I was able to stomach it myself. Now I loved it, and she began making one for me. She was spreading the mustard when she tipped her head toward the sound of the newscaster explaining that five thousand paratroopers with fixed bayonets were on patrol in Baltimore.

"He takes no pleasure in being right about what was going to happen if black people kept pushing. I know we can't blame this on Dr. King, but he was playing with fire. Everyone's gone crazy." She took a drag from her cigarette and exhaled. "I can't imagine what this must be like for his widow."

We were about to sit in the kitchen bombarded by the TV when I suggested we eat in her studio. On the way she asked how my painting was going. It wasn't that unusual: She was a painter as well. She'd taken it up the year before the divorce. Sigrun once asked me if I'd started painting in order to get closer to my mom. I thought that was ridiculous, but it was true that it was becoming the glue that held us together. I told Mom about my 19th and 20th century art history class, explaining that I thought the changes in the way reality was portrayed by the Expressionists through the Cubists were as radical as the changes we were going through now.

Without planning to, I asked, "Have you ever considered taking LSD?"

"Can I assume you have?" she asked.

"Yes," I smiled, "as well as natural psychedelics like psilocybin and mescaline." I took a swallow of buttermilk and admired the abstract map that it left on the side of the glass.

"After the divorce, just before I moved back to Palm Springs from Los Angeles, I met someone who'd taken LSD with a psychiatrist named Oscar Janiger. He ran experiments with hundreds of people until a few years ago. I've since met artists here in the desert who've taken it. They mostly spoke very highly of it, so it doesn't surprise me that you'd be interested in all that." She ate some of her sandwich before adding, "I did ask Dr. Kirsch, the Jungian therapist I saw in LA, about it. He was quite wary of the whole idea. Ultimately, I decided that I've spent too long putting my ego together to take a chance on something that might unravel it."

"You mean you're afraid you'd have a bad trip?"

"If by that you mean I'm concerned I'd lose my sense of self and the perspective I've attained, then yes. I paid…" She hesitated for a moment before adding, "We all paid a heavy price for my therapeutic journey. It wouldn't be worth risking it." That was as close as she had ever come to acknowledging the effect of the divorce and her leaving town since I declined her offer to see a therapist when I was eleven.

I couldn't think of anything to say, and we ate in silence until she pulled out two recent paintings and asked my opinion. One I liked and explained why. "This other one," I said, "has no energy or passion. It's been overworked." She'd heard blunt criticism from me before, but didn't mind. It was the same reason I sought her feedback about my paintings. In this area we allowed ourselves complete honesty.

I indicated that I needed to head back to LA. She walked me out and admired how I'd built out my van. A psychedelic poster advertising a show with Blue Cheer at the Shrine Auditorium lay on the bed. "Should I be concerned about you taking psychedelics?" she asked.

"No, Mom. They can be overwhelming, but in a good way... humbling and exhilarating at the same time. Actually, the biggest challenge is handling the divide between the extraordinary world revealed in those spirit drugs and what's happening elsewhere," I said as I got in.

"I hope you don't get lost in either one," she said with maternal concern.

"Mom, what I mean is, you need to be careful. The situation could become dangerous, even in a little town like this."

"Paul will protect us," she said and shook her head. I could see she was both reassured and disturbed at the implications of his keeping a pistol next to their bed. She gave me a kiss good-bye and whispered, "Be safe."

On the surface, Los Angeles was peaceful. Folks in South Central LA might be angry, but the earlier Watts Riots had shown the futility of rioting in their own neighborhood. But in other parts of the country, even weeks after King's assassination, turmoil and violence continued in full view.

Scrambling to stay ahead of the rage against white America, Congress quickly passed the Civil Rights Act of 1968, including the Fair Housing Act, and LBJ signed it on the 11th of April. None of this seemed to affect the war effort. The week after King was killed, nearly 25,000 military reserves were called up to serve two-year commitments. The government promised that the total number in Vietnam would be no more than 549,500.

For many, it was a tipping point. Beginning on April 23, the student anti-war and anti-racist movements took a radical leap; no longer were they going to allow big institutions to function as usual. The most dramatic action occurred at Columbia University, where students occupied several university buildings. The white students, led by SDS, were protesting the university's institutional support of the war in Vietnam through its Institute for Defense Analyses (IDA), a front for the Department of Defense. The black students opposed a planned gymnasium, condemning it as part of the university's racist treatment of the Harlem community on its eastern border. Joined by their outrage but separated by their different agendas, the students soon divided into white and black factions and occupied different buildings. Throughout a long, tumultuous week, the black students, with tremendous support from the surrounding Harlem community that had recently seen riots in response to King's assassination, kept their occupation peaceful. Ultimately, Columbia University canceled the gymnasium. The white occupation was much more destructive of Columbia University property, and generated violence but no deaths. In the end the university disaffiliated itself from IDA. The protests were seen around the world. The establishment media showed it from the outside, and a growing underground media caught the action from within the occupied buildings.

Scarcely had this moved to the back pages of the newspapers when, in the first week of May, French students in Paris, angered at university closures and threatened expulsions, took to the streets to protest their treatment, capitalism, and repression in general. Support for them grew. Labor unions and others joined in, and a general strike brought France to a halt on May 22. French President de Gaulle disappeared from public view while France swung wildly between anarchism and revolution.

In spite of this mayhem, beginning May 10, in Paris, peace talks had begun between the North Vietnamese and the United States.

Talks of peace were complicated by the fact that Johnson allowed his B-52s to continue to bomb North Vietnam. He said it was intended to force them to negotiate and agree to our terms. The North Vietnamese demanded that the bombing had to stop before serious discussions could take place. LBJ refused and said that they had to first begin a reciprocal de-escalation in South Vietnam.

Another problem that bedeviled the negotiations was the same problem that started our involvement in Vietnam: Western governments had "provisionally" separated Vietnam since 1956. Since then the United States had propped up the South to thwart unification with the communists in North Vietnam. In effect, Vietnam was in a civil war, with the U.S. doing the majority of the fighting for the South and the Soviet Union arming the North. President Thieu of South Vietnam didn't recognize the North Vietnamese government as legitimate and vice versa, so they certainly didn't want to give each other an official seat at peace talks aiming to unite their country. The participants couldn't even find agreement on the shape of a table for their meeting. And all around them, Paris was in convulsions.

I called Stanley and asked him to come by with more "product." He showed up waving some papers. "That motherfucker Martin's got more balls dead than most cats have when they're alive." He handed me a joint of some "good shit" he'd brought for me to try. "Can't say his nonviolence has a candle's chance in the shit storm we're in, but listen to what he laid down last August, right after the brothers destroyed Newark and Detroit."

In a professorial tone, he began to read from Dr. King's *The Crisis in America's Cities*: "'Mass civil disobedience can use rage as a constructive and creative force. It is purposeless to tell Negroes they should not be enraged when they should be. Indeed, they will be mentally healthier if they do not suppress rage but vent it constructively and use its energy peacefully but forcefully to cripple the operations of an oppressive society.'"

Stanley laughed sardonically as he took another hit. "No wonder I'm so motherfuckin' healthy," he exhaled. "My therapy was trying to 'cripple the operations of an oppressive society' during our riot number one right here in Watts."

"What makes me so sure that you were more into the forceful than the peaceful part of that?" I said.

"We were ahead of our time in 1965, just waiting for the other niggers to catch up."

I winced at the term and Stanley looked at me soberly. I asked him, "What happens if I use that word, just kidding around?" and handed him the beer we had been sharing.

"It's never going to be funny. You put me in my black bag and I'm liable to slice your honky ass like a Virginia ham."

"You're not in your black bag now?"

"Hell no, man. We're just shooting the shit. Listen, if Bobby Kennedy could tell it straight to King, I figure other white folk know how."

"What's this got to do with Bobby Kennedy?"

"Man, I got all sorts of friends. Some of my lawyer contacts back east told me that after Kennedy read this," and here he shook King's article he'd read from, "he and Marian Wright Edelman and a few others suggested Dr. King lead some poor people to D.C. and camp out there until poverty took back some of the headlines from the goddamn war."

"No shit? I never heard about that."

"I doubt Bobby and the others held a press conference to announce they'd suggested a fucking sit-in of the whole capital." He chuckled. "These motherfuckers been playing a high-stakes game. I can't say I hold out much hope for it but... Hell, man, think about it: Six weeks after Martin is killed, his wife and his people at SCLC are knocking at the gates of the White House. They got a fucking shantytown called Resurrection City with three thousand poor folks demanding, 'Feed the people! Get us some real jobs!'"

He got up and walked around for a while, looking at my paintings in the dying light. "I never told you but my dad 'bout wore out that book on dada and surrealism you gave him."

"Great. Not many people have a dad into dada."

He chuckled and continued in a quiet voice. "Last night I saw a Cuban documentary about how the North Vietnamese handle the B-52 bombing raids on Hanoi. They hide in skinny holes in the ground with all hell breaking loose above them, and as soon as the siren signals that the planes have gone, they jump out by the thousands and start helping the injured and cleaning shit up. The narrator repeated over and over, 'Hatred into energy. Hatred into energy.' You just know those motherfuckers are never going to give up."

"Put that together with Resurrection City and it's enough to give you hope that things might actually turn out okay," I said.

"I doubt it," he replied. "And I'll tell you something unknown to most whites except undercover agents: There's a lot going on that isn't in the news."

I looked at him questioningly.

"The Black Panther Party's got a Southern California office, and they're telling it like it is out on the street. And you know they aren't talking nonviolence when the police come into the ghetto."

"You signed up?"

"No, no, they're pulling in the Vietnam vets and the gangbangers, talking about educating the 'lumpenproletariat' brothers for the battles that are coming. Anyway, they'd disapprove of my businesses and, you know, a man's got to eat." He took the ten dollars I'd put on the table for the lid I was buying and smiled. "I'm just another middle-class nigger helping to finance the motherfuckers." He shoved his fist into the air in a black power salute and whispered conspiratorially as he split, "Free Huey! Off the Pig!"

So I'm helping to finance the financier, I thought, sitting there in the twilight of my innocence. The idea made me uncomfortable, but not particularly bad. It was complicated, like everything else that was swirling around.

Two weeks later, shortly after midnight on June 5, 1968, I was coming up for air after hours of being deep into painting. I flicked on the radio and caught coverage of the results of the California Democratic primary. Only ten minutes down Wilshire Boulevard from my studio, Bobby Kennedy had just given his victory speech. I felt an electric surge of possibility. At the last minute, I'd voted for him in spite of all my doubts. He was hope incarnate, the only anti-war candidate who could overcome the Democratic machine and the lackluster Hubert Humphrey. Humphrey, as LBJ's vice president, was fatally tied to the morass in Vietnam and controversial civil rights. Even to his fans he was seen as a neutered lackey.

So now what? Bobby versus Richard Nixon, the same sleaze-bag who lost to Bobby's brother in 1960? It sure seemed possible that Bobby could reassure scared and angry whites, as well as get the blacks working the precincts instead of burning them down. He'd send Nixon back under a slimy rock where he belonged. The Kennedy clan would stage the biggest family comeback in American politics. Our trauma of five years ago would be healed by the grace of a democratic system that had stumbled but not fallen.

There were a lot of ifs and suppositions, but I couldn't stop from singing and doing a little jig around the studio as the radio droned on in the background. Suddenly, after only a few steps on that long road toward what his victory in California made a reasonable wish instead of some stoned fantasy, a disembodied voice interrupted me to say that Bobby had been shot. I soon learned that a twenty-four-year-old fanatic, obsessed over Bobby's support for Israel, had put a bullet into Bobby's brain with a dinky .22-caliber pistol. In less than a day, the last, best chance for national redemption was dead. What little faith and hope that remained in my heart bled out onto the kitchen floor of the Ambassador Hotel.

10

REALITY SPLINTERS

I tried not to think. I got so drunk I threw up. I got stoned and slept and ached for more sleep. Even before Martin and Bobby were blown away, I wasn't sure I believed in the electoral process or trusted that Bobby Kennedy could make a difference. But I liked that they were there, trying, believing. They were the middle ground and it had been washed away.

Our master dreamers were dead. JFK had stirred up a lot of hopes. Martin had dreamed of a racially integrated and unified America. And Bobby had repeated countless times: "Some men see things as they are and say why. I dream things that never were and say why not."

Here was why not: Either some random son-of-a-bitch or a whole conspiracy was going to gun you down and turn your dream into our nightmare. It made a compelling argument for armed revolution.

The ringing phone pierced my fog of depression and angry helplessness. "I can't be alone," Beth intoned. "Can I come over?"

I resisted. "Look," I began…

"I was there, Dennis, I was there!" Tightly wrapped hysteria surged through her voice. "I was at the Ambassador!"

"How did…" I began, but she wasn't listening.

"My aunt worked on his campaign and she really wanted me to come to the victory party. She said it was going to be an historical event." Her voice shredded into weeping. "I can't handle this…I can't even fucking vote," she managed to say through her tears, "I—I talked to friends but I—I don't want to be alone."

"I can't imagine how horrible…but look, Beth…"

More gently this time, she interrupted again. "Dennis, you were a real jerk, but you were right."

"Jerk?" I questioned.

"Kicking me out so suddenly was cruel, but what you said was true. It just took me a while to accept it."

"I didn't handle it very well," I admitted.

She took that for a yes and said she was on her way.

I experienced another facet of sex shortly after she burst through my door: a salve that provides temporary amnesia. We didn't make love; we weren't creative or even particularly sexy. It was rough, almost savage, and it went on and on with an intensity that obliterated thought. Eventually the coupling that began in desperation ended with tenderness and exhausted sleep. When we came to, she began catching me up on her life.

"Not long after you broke us up, my parents urged me to go to temple, if only to get me to stop crying and out of the house. I felt I had to since they were paying for school and getting me an apartment. But it didn't turn out quite like they had imagined. I met this group of Hasidim who introduced me to the stories and teachings of the Baal Shem Tov. It's a very spiritual and metaphysically oriented Judaism. It's really tripped my parents out, but I know you'd love it."

Something in her tone put me back in Catechism class.

"We are all manifestations of God, Dennis," she purred as she cuddled in my arms. "God is with us, so there is never any reason to fear."

I smelled fundamentalism. "How do you explain what happened at the Ambassador?" I asked as calmly as I could, then quickly added, "Where is your God in this time of madness?"

"Believe me, we've talked about it a lot. Avi, one of the leaders, told a Rabbi Nachman story of a king who was warned by his advisors that a plague or curse was coming. The grain would be tainted and all who ate it would go mad. They wanted him to put up a secret store of grain so they could remain sane. But the king said, 'No, we will eat the tainted grain. But we will also put a mark on each of our foreheads to recognize each other so that when the madness descends, we will be reminded that there was a time when we were not mad and that there will come a time when we are no longer mad.'"

I laughed. "And in the meantime, fuck your brains out?"

She sat up and covered her breasts with one arm, suddenly embarrassed by her nakedness. "Jews don't have the same hang-ups about sex as you poor Catholics."

"For which I, a budding atheist, gladly proclaim, thank God! He didn't screw everybody up the same way."

"Don't you get it, Dennis? We just have to stick together and have faith. We are the link between God and all creation."

I groaned. "Have you seen Warren and Heidi lately? They're so deep into Jesus that they both can't wait to tell me how I can be saved whenever I run into them—which is rare, fortunately. But you should go see them. You could argue over which God will get credit for salvation when it comes." I rolled off the mattress to the ladder and climbed down.

Beth followed me down and quickly dressed. "I really thought you were open-minded, but you're as uptight and conventional as my parents."

"Beth, seeing you and having sex with you was a welcome time-out. And if that story and those people also help you get through this craziness, I guess that's cool. But I don't think that grabbing onto some religious dogma, even airy-fairy spiritual dogma, is a liberating move. I once believed in God, and as comforting as it can seem, I see it now as a place of desperation and fantasy."

The slamming door was her response. It occurred to me that she'd come over simply to be able to be the one who left. That I could believe.

I withdrew into my studio and painted. When I'd returned to California, my painting had freed up along with my mind and body. Doing my own thing had meant painting bold, abstract explosions across big canvases, largely in black and white. Painting each one was like a wrestling match, tacitly encouraged by others who had previously explored this terrain. Jackson Pollock had a similar energy, but my pieces had more in common with Franz Klein, Robert Motherwell, and Hans Hoffman. Gradually, over two years, I had included hints of recognizable space—corners, doors, shafts of light, or a suggestion of a body. I thought of them as "inscapes": abstracted, interior landscapes both architectural and psychological.

I experimented with expanding physical boundaries, moving from two to three dimensions by building a small room out of four-by-eight-feet plywood walls. One could enter and become a figure within that inscape. I also began to develop photographs on two-by-three-feet canvases, which I then painted on. However shaky everything else felt, I was secure in my work. The world could go to hell without me.

I dug deep into the history of art and discovered it explained, if not predicted, the future. Since the 1700s, the Industrial Revolution had spread out of control, altering the natural landscape and upending humanity's notion of time and work. In the same period, humanistic ideas came of age. The Enlightenment generated experiments with democracy that forced radical political changes on the western world, most notably the goals of equality and individual rights in the American Revolution. Painting also moved from its roots in religious allegory, portraits, and landscapes, and in the 1860s, it began to challenge the very idea of what constituted reality.

As I neared completion of my MFA, I prepared a presentation for my class in the history of 19th and 20th century European art designed to show that the collapse of a common ground that we were experiencing now had begun one hundred years earlier. Around that time science and technology, two high-spirited offspring of Industrialism and the Enlightenment, developed photography. That freed painters from having to record how things looked. Western artists were no longer wedded to one version of reality, or commenting on it via allegory and metaphor. They were free to follow their own way of seeing. Within a few short years, certain painters had refocused the art world from a super-realistic Neo-Classicism style to their impression of reality, Impressionism.

Most critics and traditional artists were outraged and disparaged this visual blasphemy by labeling further experimentation with more "isms": Post-Impressionism, Expressionism, Fauvism, and Cubism. Whatever its name, it was challenging the nature of reality right in front of the public's eyes. These painters were capturing previously unseen truths about our world. The Cubists—Picasso and Braque especially—shattered any illusion that reality was solid and coherent. They broke their subjects into a carnival of shattered pieces. It couldn't exist, and yet it was recognizable. Their work might have been written off as insane, except in the same moment Einstein confirmed the essence of their vision with the theory of relativity: physical mass could turn into energy...and back again. This was reality too, impossible according to the old Newtonian way of thinking, and artists were reflecting how it might look and feel. Only sixty years prior to our summer of 1968, these artistic and mathematical worlds that had been previously invisible to our eye and, as Freud argued at that time, to our consciousness, had been revealed.

As reality was further abstracted in art, its ineffable quality was compounded by the emotional horror of World War I and II and the Holocaust. Then, the blinding actualization of the theory of relativity was revealed in the explosions of the atomic bomb. As the irradiated dust from Hiroshima and Nagasaki settled over us, our wordless horror and awe found form in Abstract Expressionism. This art—along with the Beatniks, Black music, and Elvis—was the avenue by which "Do your own thing" infiltrated and became American culture. I began to see myself as part of a lineage of artists and pioneers, the avant-garde, who stood at the forefront of radical social and cultural change.

"To thine own self be true" and "Do your own thing" were in full bloom, and I set out to capture how this moment had evolved in an experiential, multimedia art piece. If I had any religion, this was it. I couldn't get Jefferson Airplane and a psychedelic light show into the classroom, but I did figure out a way to disorient and entertain my fellow students, all the while informing them of the historical continuum they were part of.

Mike was more than happy to blow people's minds and helped me manage the audio tape player, two turntables and two film projectors that I needed to pull this off. The classroom setting was far from inspiring, but once the forty students had settled into their seats, we closed the blinds and turned off the lights. In the dim light, I began a tape of a man's voice that gently suggested that everyone close his or her eyes, breathe slowly, and relax. Then he suggested they let their hands fall to their sides and feel the tingling of their blood. A solo Japanese flute began playing as the voice directed their attention to the sensations in their hands, both the pulsing weight and a peculiar lightness. They could, if they wished, allow one or both hands to slowly rise. As I expected, I saw in the dim light that far more than half of the students were soon having that experience.

After the voice brought their awareness back to themselves sitting in their chairs, it gave way to Debussy's "Prelude to the Afternoon of a Faun" as two slide projectors displayed paintings beginning with the Neo-Classicism of the 1860s and moving into the 20th century. The Japanese flute was replaced by a woman's voice, which began to explain the manner in which the art movements of the last hundred years had, with the aid of physics and psychology, come to depict multiple and simultaneous realities. As the slides provided visual evidence of this evolution, Debussy was interrupted by Igor Stravinsky's "Firebird Suite," which matched the wild colors of the Fauvists' paintings.

The taped lecture gave way to a jazz piece, John Handy at the Monterey Jazz Festival, as the slides ended with images of the unmistakable mushroom cloud. A projector began to show a short film of people in animal masks dancing ceremoniously in the coastal Ballona

Wetlands. The Stravinsky dropped out and the Buffalo Springfield declared, *"There's something happening here, but what it is ain't exactly clear,"* as another projector showing the same characters filmed from a different point of view began to compete for one's visual attention. This song and the jazz overlapped until the film reels emptied and the class was left to gaze at photos of our galaxy taken by recently lofted satellites as the haunting *"Stop, hey, what's that sound? Everybody look what's going down,"* repeated over and over. All that was left at the end was the sound of the film tails flapping over and over against the projectors. It was as trippy as I could make it without putting acid in the school's drinking fountains.

USC was a notoriously "straight" campus. While many students may have tried grass, I knew from my time there that psychedelics and other aspects of this Cultural Revolution that was unfolding were still too "far out" for most of them. But, except for two jocks who stormed out saying it was bullshit, they took my little trip and loved it. I felt I had done my bit for a better future.

It wasn't clear what the teacher, an emigrant from Eastern Europe, thought until the next class when he announced to us, "Your generation thinks it's special, unique, but it's not. These times are interesting, but there have been many dangerously complicated and overwhelming times throughout history, as recently as the Nazi threat and World War II, which formed the basis for many of the stories of my own youth. But understand this," he said solemnly, "anyone who doesn't have a way of explaining what is going on is certain to be emotionally overwhelmed and wither. Until newspapers or neighborhood gossip or your own mind make sense of it, there is often a house of mirrors aspect to the present moment."

"Do you think that's why people make art?" a young woman asked.

"Yes, but it's more elemental than that. We humans are, above all, a storytelling species. Concocting a story to make sense of things is the only way we can get to sleep at night. It makes no difference how many twists and turns, changes, or negations of the basic assumptions a story suffers; we need story. You may feel powerless in it, or you may feel empowered to change its direction. But, regardless of what story you come up with, you and every other human will find a story. Madness is a people without a story."

"Just because you tell a story doesn't mean it's true," a student declared.

"Unfortunately, that doesn't lessen its power. For example, the Nazi's told stories about the Jews that were not true, but for a time they prevailed. Truth is experiential, like the different views of a bowl of apples. Truth is relative, and just because your version or your story doesn't prevail doesn't make it false."

Someone else asked, "What if the people can't agree what the story is?"

He thought for a moment before answering, "Consider that only thirty years ago, Picasso communicated the shattered realities of the Spanish Civil War when he painted the experience of the aerial bombing of the village of Guernica. He did this not only as a protest, but also as a way to tell the story, however horrible, and to begin to make sense out of the overwhelming emotions evoked by that event. The fact that he created a masterpiece but his side still lost the war to the fascists is just one story we tell ourselves. For me, the bombing of the village of Guernica was a tragedy, but the painting is a victory. For the fascists of Spain and Germany, the opposite is true."

He looked at us with sad eyes, evidence of his own story churning inside his mind. "Competing narratives is life. That, I would suggest, is one thing that hasn't changed over the millennia." He perked up a bit and aimed his final comments to me. "Mr. Hicks is to be commended for capturing how this has evolved in our modern era in a vivid yet thoughtful fashion. Excellent job."

I walked out elated and relieved to find support for my history lesson, my narrative; the whole world was like a Cubist painting. But my satisfaction was ephemeral; there's only so much enjoyment you can get from describing the asylum you live in.

Dramatically different narratives about revolution and radical change were competing in that moment. We began to get reports that the Red Guard in China—the legions of young, fervent communists Mao had set free to do a course correction for his revolution—had begun to turn in their parents to the authorities to be tried, and perhaps killed, for being counterrevolutionaries. In one way it was easy to recognize the spirit of their movement. The admonition "Don't trust anyone over thirty!" had spread rapidly across the land after first being declared during the Free Speech Movement in Berkeley back in 1964. It was obvious that challenging old ways of thinking was the essence of radical change. But it was hard to believe that the "pigs" were your parents. As various friends agreed, they might be clueless, but they were rarely dangerous.

Furthermore, we had to question whether those articles stressing Mao's madness were even true. Believing them rested on accepting the establishment press. It was in this government's interest to plant doubts that China's experiment in building a socialist society was succeeding and, like reports that we were winning in Vietnam, it could all be CIA misinformation. In the alternative papers and magazines, of which there were many, Maoism was a beacon, not a dead end. Still, it was hard to be too confident about any version of socialism. The Soviet Union's fairy tale of a socialist paradise had turned very scary. The "Prague Spring" in Czechoslovakia made a crack in the Iron Curtain, and on August 20, 1968, the Soviets invaded with 750,000 troops and 6,500 tanks to fill it. This wasn't our government's anti-communist propaganda. This crackdown wrote "The End" to this experiment in democracy in a socialist country. I was still no Marxist, but this was not good news for the socialist path to equality and freedom.

Meanwhile, to further add to the general uncertainty and craziness, the Pope condemned birth control as the Catholics continued their fantasy that sex was mainly for procreation. Mike called it "an obvious plot to increase the number of Catholics and take over the universe." The plain truth was that liberated attitudes toward sex freaked people out. Right-wing politicians like Strom Thurmond of South Carolina condemned pornography, and California Governor Ronald Reagan declared there were orgies going on during demonstrations. It was true that bras were being burnt at the same rate as draft cards. Nipples, those taboo buds of life, could be seen bouncing along damn near anywhere. That had to drive those old men crazy.

Less than three months after Bobby was assassinated, the Democratic National Convention met in Chicago. Three kinds of young people went to protest. They were all anti-war and mostly white, but the agreement stopped there. The "McCarthy kids" knew they couldn't get Eugene McCarthy nominated, but they wanted to tie Hubert Humphrey or whoever was nominated to a strong anti-war plank. They were working within the system, for now. Many SDS and "Mobe kids" (National Mobilization Committee to End the War in Vietnam) had had enough of the system. It was time for a revolution to bring about racial equality and a new sort of America. What they needed were more revolutionaries to join them, and the spectacle of cops or troops cracking down on all-American white kids exercising their constitutional rights was sure to convince young, middle America to join the cause of freedom and equality. The last contingent was the "Yippies," a non-group inspired by Groucho Marxism. They were visitors from the cultural and chemical revolutions that were going on across the U.S. Though without official leaders, there were two spokesmen for these cultural anarchists, Abbie Hoffman and Jerry Rubin. Their hyperbolic answer to an intolerable reality was to overthrow it. They approached life as theatre of the absurd, a continuously present moment spiced up with free love, occasional jolts of acid, and a carefree, "Fuck you!" attitude.

Competing narratives, for sure. A part of me could be found in all three overlapping movements. After some agonizing, I decided to try to boycott politics, but like the war in Vietnam, the whole spectacle was on TV. I didn't own one, but I was in a beer bar with friends and we watched protestors breaking windows as police teargassed, chased, and beat them mercilessly. Another time I saw police with nightsticks going onto the floor of the Democratic Convention and pushing people around. Even the commentators agreed it was insane. Chicago's Mayor Daley had silenced the voices of opposition by taking the law into his own hands. Hubert Humphrey was left to put the pieces of the Democratic Party back together.

My friend Jaimo called me collect from a Chicago jail. He hadn't been able to reach his grandma, the one who'd nearly had her head cracked at the Century City demonstration, but he knew she'd bail him out. He practically begged me to keep calling her until I reached her. "No way were we going to let the system do business as usual. But the Chicago pigs were lying in wait. They brought the war home, and they are playing for keeps. They won't even let me see a doctor."

I finally reached Jaimo's grandmother. After she collected the basic information and said she'd deal with it, she asked me why I hadn't protested. I made some excuse, but she would have none of it. "This was your *Kristallnacht*, young man, the moment in 1938 that the Nazis officially began targeting the Jewish shop owners and upper class. Now the Chicago Gestapo has proven they won't stop with targeting the blacks. They already arrested some of the leaders, your Chicago 8, for opposing their imperialist war. You better believe this is the beginning of a police state and fascism. Mark my words, they've got their man in Dick Nixon!"

I answered that if things were that bad, protesting didn't seem like it would do much. She was silent for a beat and then said, "Well, then you must find some other way to be effective. Passivity is a crime, and naïveté is no excuse."

She was one far-out, pissed-off old lady, and I couldn't disagree with her, but I hadn't yet figured out what the hell being "effective" would mean for me. So, I continued to ferment. I had lots of company.

Only a week later about a hundred and fifty women rose up in protest as Atlantic City hosted the Miss America Pageant. They made it clear to a male-dominated world that they would no longer quietly accept the exploitation of women. Personally, I had no argument with the women's liberation movement. Even though it came at my own emotional expense when I was little, I supported my mother's leaving my dad to find herself. To me, there was no good argument against feminism.

In Mexico City a student-led protest in Tlatelolco Square was met with thunderous violence, and hundreds of demonstrators were killed and injured. Just weeks later at the Olympics in Mexico City, two black American athletes, Tommie Smith and John Carlos, brought the Black Power movement into the world of international sports by raising their fists on the victory stand. It appeared that people across the globe, especially the young, were fed up with the status quo.

But that didn't mean there was no normalcy. The beleaguered city of Detroit finally had cause for celebration as the Tigers beat the St. Louis Cardinals four games to three in the World Series. Economically, people were okay. The average annual income was almost $8,000, and the average cost of a new home was $15,000. Even Jackie Kennedy got her life back to some kind of normal by marrying a Greek shipping tycoon, Aristotle Onassis.

It may have looked to some that American democracy was working. We were still free to decide who our leaders were. But as far as many of us were concerned, the choice had been made irrelevant through reactionary violence. Even if you believed that voting made a difference, Nixon and Humphrey, the two candidates, were both terrible choices. My mother, who for all her proto-feminist values was, I suspected, a closet Republican, said that Nixon was a liar. But he was a talented liar, and his call to America's "silent majority" to help him uphold "law and order" had him tied in the polls with Humphrey. Just days before the election, LBJ tried to throw the contest to Humphrey by announcing a suspension of "all air, naval, and artillery bombardment of North Vietnam" as of November 1. However, in spite of giving up the presidency so he could concentrate on making peace, LBJ was unable to convince the South Vietnamese government to negotiate with the North Vietnamese. Their intransience meant that the Democrats, though they had been promising it for months, were unable to announce an end to this war that had so divided this country.

With the Democrats so obviously ineffective, and our real leaders assassinated, America finally invited Tricky Dick into the White House.

1968 was overwhelming for many reasons. Many of us were convinced that America's elected leaders had deserted the spirit and goals of the Constitution and embraced becoming an empire. It was clear to me that the trembling kid who had tried to explain to an Army shrink why he didn't want to go to war had been vindicated. The Vietnam War—and all it represented—was a bad idea. To be sure, that was a hard narrative for a freedom-loving people to live with. Many Americans, and a majority of the voters, had consumed the poisoned grain, and we were now living with the madness it produced. At the same time, many of us had a terrible feeling that Nixon was the perfect man for those times…and as 1968 came to an end, he was only getting started.

11

REVOLUTION

During that chaotic fall of 1968, as America slowly tilted toward Nixon, I finished my MFA. Along with getting into photography, Mike and I had played around with an old sixteen-millimeter Bell and Howell camera that had belonged to my mom's father. Up in the mountains we shot *Koan,* a short film that explored the shifting nature of identity. I was after the visual equivalent of the sound of one hand clapping. It was shown at rock concerts in the Shrine auditorium as part of a light show run by friends, known as the Single Wing Turquoise Bird. It was thrilling to dance with hundreds of others to Pink Floyd and other bands while our black-and-white film was flickering through a swirl of colors projected on the high screens surrounding us.

Everything was groovy if I looked at the world in a certain light. I had a future as a painter. I'd sold my first big painting for $300. I was encouraged to think I was good, possibly better than that. A serious career beckoned. But to spend my time in the studio painting meant not directly engaging with what was going on outside, which felt immoral and cowardly. My society was coming apart, and something had to replace it. I was an artist; what could be more creative than to join in changing it? I'd come too far to hide out in another cave of delusions like the guilty Catholic boy I'd once been. I had confronted being condemned to Hell and had left the Church; I had stared down the draft board; I had fucked myself free from sexual repression; I had discovered extraordinary versions of reality and a profound spirituality.

Painting came from a deeply felt vision within me and satisfied a personal desire and need. I loved it, but it wasn't enough to live just for myself. I was ready to abandon my burgeoning career because to stay inside and paint seemed masturbatory. The outside world beckoned. There were countless images on film and TV that showed how terrible this war was. Those images of the agonies and folly of war had turned many against it. In that sense, TV revealed the new Guernica. It was time to make a difference in the world outside my studio, but how?

Chairman Mao said in his Little Red Book that political power came through the barrel of a gun. There was talk in the air about white radicals taking up arms. I wasn't ready to sign up for that, but it didn't seem too much of a Maoist stretch to add that support for radical political change came from a pen and the barrel of a lens.

Mike was working on a feature film script about a bunch of white kids who had become terrorists. It was to be shot like a documentary. The problem was that Mike's writing was mostly a string of intriguing, occasionally hilarious non-sequiturs. Making sense was secondary to humor and momentary insight. The connecting thread was a spirit of Zen anarchism, a Yippie fantasy that reflected Mike's devout rejection of any theoretical or ideological framework. It was revolution as a "happening," or a "granfallon" as Kurt Vonnegut would say, a collection of interesting scenes that didn't quite cohere or pay off with a dramatic finish. This was how Mike saw the world. And he did have a point: The extraordinary events of the previous year or two seemed as close to the bizarre and disconnected scenes he'd imagined as they did to some consistent narrative as my art history professor had suggested.

One afternoon Stanley came by when Mike was there, and Mike asked him to read about twenty pages of the script. He did and then tossed it down as he announced, "Man, this is a jive-ass piece of shit.

These motherfucking white kids are just playing at revolution—like it was Easter week in Palm Springs with guns. You can't be fuckin' serious…" he sputtered to a stop and glared at Mike.

"I wouldn't have thought satire was foreign to black humor," Mike replied calmly.

"Motherfucker, you know I work at the USC film department, and you think all I know is how black people think?"

"No," Mike said, "but I think it would be racist if I didn't take your race into account."

Stanley took a breath. "If you're saying I lost my sense of humor, you be right, as we black folks say. But you better know you're gonna piss off a lot of people who take revolution seriously."

"Hell, I take it seriously," Mike said. "That's the reason to fuck with the whole concept of revolution; make people think about it from all angles. Haven't you seen *La Chinoise?*"

"Man, you think you're some sort of American Godard?" Stanley grinned with genuine astonishment. "Well, I'd say you're more like a Midwestern Fellini. But anything is possible for a white man. I'll tell you this—you better be one fine editor or you're going to make *Gidget* seem like high art. And seriously, do not thank me in the credits." He laughed his way out the door.

Mike was undeterred and soon asked if I wanted to help write, direct, produce, and act in what would amount to a cubist movie. It was an offer I should have resisted. I knew I'd be the bank for some of this folly, but I thought I could find a way to hold it all together. The chaos and madness of the last year had put revolution in the air. I felt driven to make some sort of comment on our explosive times. Also, Mike and I had a variety of friends who were in film school and would help. We were always going to movies and dissecting them afterward. Making one didn't seem like an impossible task.

So, I held my breath and jumped. The film was to be made on the cheap in black and white, and no one was getting paid. I found a used Moviola editing machine and got a great deal on a used sixteen-millimeter Arriflex camera and lenses from a documentary filmmaker who was moving up the ladder in Hollywood. In the fall of '68, we began shooting.

By this time my beard was scraggly and my hair cascaded past my shoulders, perfect for a revolutionary icon. Barely more than a year had passed since the CIA in Bolivia had chased down Che Guevara. I mentioned that the photo of a dead but beatific Che flooded the world as a warning. But the image was also used for a far different effect on posters that showed it along with his extraordinary claim, "The true revolutionary is motivated by love." Che was pure, uncompromised even by criticisms of the Cuban Revolution. Furthermore, Che looked like paintings of Jesus, and his martyrdom recast the Christ story: a true revolutionary who sacrificed his life for the poor of the world. Who could resist that tale?

Though some part of me expected to be struck by lightning, nonetheless I dressed in a thin, gauzy robe. We found all sorts of mini-dramas as we drove the streets and freeways, filming out the sliding side door of my VW van. I interviewed a variety of people about their take on what was going on in the world: who was wrong, and what needed to be done. Folks were thoughtful, whether outraged or sad. We also filmed demonstrations and things exploding and burning off the TV.

Threaded through these scenes was the story, such as it was, that involved two "urban guerillas" who were in hiding after bombing a corporate office and a military recruitment center. Beth and I had settled into a friendship, and we filmed her and her new boyfriend swimming naked at a "safe house," my dad's cabin in the mountains. Sex and revolution—who could resist?

Mike and I knew that rich liberals in Hollywood and New York were helping to fund the Black Panthers. So we created a mysterious, masked Mr. Big: a corporate boss who was the money behind our guerilla warfare, effectively playing both sides of the game. We plucked dialogue out of the caldron of current events, and nothing we came up with seemed further out than the outrageous stories in the establishment and alternative newspapers. The problem was that there was nothing sparking our characters' revolutionary fervor except that the government and the system were beyond salvation. I kept thinking that there had to be some vision of the future that rationalized bombing and "offing the motherfucking pigs."

"Revolution comes from rage, not some higher chakra," Mike insisted, and after we saw *Bonnie and Clyde*, he was unstoppable. "There it is in brutal slow motion, man. Violence has always had a free pass in Hollywood, while nudity is outlawed. Guns, yes; dicks, no!" he laughed.

But even before we got anywhere near a rough cut, it became obvious that the implication of our film was that revolution came out of the air, randomly, by chance. We might as well have said it occurred because the stars were in the proper alignment. It cheapened the idea of revolution, made it seem less serious than it deserved. We might be able to live life as one ongoing "happening," but revolution wasn't some "petit bourgeois art project" as one friend said after viewing a few scenes. *Little White Whiskers at His Age* died prematurely.

Mike claimed he didn't mind: Just writing and filming what we had was success enough. I was pissed off at him for being so cavalier about the money and effort we'd wasted, but I knew it was my own damn fault. I was frustrated and tired of my own naïveté. At the same time I realized that our effort was just one of many calls for revolution that echoed through the smoky ruins of 1968. Millions of people, especially the young, were in love with her. We each described her in our own way and imagined how it would be with her according to what we felt was missing. She went by one name, but she had many faces.

I remained plagued by the feeling that leading my life as usual was a tacit form of support for racism and imperialism. What next? Go back to sleep with Mr. Jones? Take acid? Escape into the wilderness? Enjoy marathons of stoned sex? Meditate? No matter what, I eventually had to come back to an unchanged world. March against the war? Confront bigots? Demonstrate for civil rights? That hadn't accomplished anything but placating laws and promises that changed nothing. It seemed that hope was nothing but a Petri dish in which frustration and rage grew like molds.

※

Culver Nichols, an old, family friend from Palm Springs and a big fan of my paintings, asked if he could take my entire Master of Fine Arts show and hang the thirteen big pieces for an indefinite period at his real estate office. It was an odd setting, but the office had once been an art gallery with great track lighting and plenty of space. It meant I could show and possibly sell my work while I decided if I was going to continue painting. It also meant I didn't need to keep my studio amidst the traffic and smog of central LA. I could move out to Venice Beach and its community of artists, beatniks, and old Jews, as I'd been thinking.

In an unofficial salute to the end of 1968, that cubist monster of a year, and possibly my painting career, I threw a party at my studio. It was a great bash with a big crowd flowing in and out. Two cops came by to see why all these people were standing around on that darkened street of commercial buildings. I was stoned but evidently convincing in my explanation, and they proved to be friendly guys with no other agenda but to keep the peace. It was a gentle farewell to this chapter of my life.

Around the same time, Mike and I went to a meeting advertised in the *Los Angeles Free Press* as a gathering for disgruntled, politicized artists and filmmakers. From what I could tell, the crowd of forty or so wanted to put their skills in support of ending the war in Vietnam or even more radical change. There was hearty agreement that we had to "do something about all the bullshit." The gathering was called by Paul Shinoff from San Francisco Newsreel, a collective of politically-oriented filmmakers who both created and distributed films that told the news from the protestors' point of view. Shinoff showed a film he had helped make about the Black Panther party in Oakland called *Off the Pig*. Less than fifteen minutes long, it managed to be a powerful declaration that these angry black men and women were serious about their legal right to openly carry guns and, if it came to it, fighting with them. Afterward, Shinoff said that the Panthers, unlike Black Nationalist groups, were Marxists and considered themselves the vanguard of the coming revolution. As such, they had always worked closely with white radicals. There was every reason to think that would continue here with the LA Panthers. Already, John Huggins, UCLA student and Deputy Minister of Information for the LA Panthers, had been active in helping to organize an LA Newsreel. San Francisco and New York Newsreels would help us get going by giving us copies of their films, as well as others on international movements made by the Cubans and North Vietnamese. Shinoff challenged us to get our act together so we could do something about this "capitalist, pig government."

From the guys I talked with that night, it was clear that some of them, though they talked a radical line, were wary of tying their film careers in any way to the Panthers. Others, graduate students in film at UCLA who knew Panthers who were studying there in a special outreach program, had no such qualms. People were clearly turned on by the tenor of the night, how through film we could pull together the various threads of the anti-war, civil rights, and cultural movements. It made a lot of sense to me too.

The events of 1968 had destroyed my trust in the American system. In spite of that, the year cruised toward an end on an optimistic, beautiful note on Christmas Eve. The first photo of our earth taken from space was sent back by the Apollo 8 astronauts as they rounded the moon on their way home. Our planet loomed over the edge of the moon, looking vulnerable in the infinite darkness yet welcoming and brimming with promise: Earthrise—the miracle of life. Perhaps this perspective would help cure our species' destructive self-centeredness. At the least, we could imagine that the earth could ride out the apparent insanity of one of its many species.

In an unexpected display of sensitivity to the fact that 1968 was a yearlong trauma and that Americans were in shock, Nixon came into office rather quietly. As 1969 dawned Nixon asked us in his inaugural address to lower our voices and pledged, "The government will listen." He reminded the nation that in early '68 he had promised he had a secret plan to end the war, and he declared, "The greatest honor history can bestow is the title of peacemaker." The press fell all over its adjectives in its attempt to trust him and believe that, as one columnist wrote, "the greatest crisis of a hundred years" was waning. The supposedly liberal media, along with the 43% who voted for him, needed to believe that this duplicitous manipulator could pull off a second coming.

Many others, myself included, had lost the faith. While Nixon was making nice, those interested in forming a Los Angeles Newsreel met again. It was a smaller group, but the fifteen who showed up were ready to make something happen. We agreed we would immediately get into showing the films we'd been given, and we collected some dues to buy two sixteen-millimeter film projectors. In a matter of days, we were ready to fulfill the dozens of requests to hold screenings at schools, SDS meetings, libraries, and union halls. We were offering evidence of real alternatives, something hard to find elsewhere. At first, I was just a projectionist, and those who'd organized the screening would talk after we'd shown the inside story of the Columbia University takeover, or how the FALN was organizing in Venezuela. In that context, I heard a Vietnam veteran, a thoughtful Marxist, and a budding feminist firebrand tell audiences their truths. All the while, I saw that people were craving to see and hear an alternative view of what was going on in the world. Many didn't believe the government, didn't trust the media, and wanted to be challenged. Taking these films out was invigorating, and in a short time, I became a confident and effective speaker, even if it wasn't clear what I was organizing people for. But that hardly seemed to matter. We didn't have to agree on the future because, whatever race they were, whatever social strata or economic class they were, they wanted to talk, they wanted information, and they wanted change.

The different kinds of protest in Chicago at the Democratic convention the previous August had dramatically proven that the anti-war movement had splintered. The Black Panther Party for Self-Defense was voicing more and more militaristic claims, and SNCC, the Student Nonviolent Coordinating Committee, had changed the N in its name to stand for "National." The civil rights movement and the doctrine of nonviolence no longer defined the black community. In East St. Louis a sniper or snipers picked off "known enemies of the black community," according to Julius Lester, a newspaper columnist and leading member of SNCC. He celebrated "this move from self-defense to aggressive action," and likened the strategy to that of the Viet Cong. Some folks in the black community were already "bringing the war back home."

As many predicted, the government was ready, even eager, for this escalation. Initially, my new "comrades" and I hadn't dealt with the Los Angeles Panthers much because their two leaders had been killed—"assassinated" was what it was called—at a meeting at UCLA on January 17, 1969. John Huggins was dead as was the charismatic Minister of Defense of the LA Panthers, Bunchy Carter. Supposedly the killers were FBI agents or members of a rival Black Nationalist organization called US, United Slaves. It was possible they were both. Obviously this was some "heavy shit," but it wasn't until I ran into Stanley that I got the inside dope.

I was running a screening at the community room of a public library on the edge of South-Central LA. I showed *Hanoi 13*, a Cuban-made film about North Vietnamese resistance, and then the Panther film *Off the Pig*. Stanley had slipped into the darkened room while the last film was on. I didn't see him until I stood at the end to address the audience. I immediately read in Stanley's eyes that I wasn't to acknowledge knowing him. I talked about how these were times of great change and that people had to organize to have a voice in that change, and handed it over to the organizer of the event. Afterward, Stanley followed me back to my camper van and jumped into the back, where we could talk without being seen.

"You gonna get your honky ass blown away if you walk around Watts talking Panther shit."

I said that the people seemed receptive to hear what white radicals and Black Panthers were up to.

"Hicks, the Panthers got all sorts of ways to get the word out, including a newspaper. You better believe that black folk are learning what the Panthers are about. The question is, do you know who Alprentice 'Bunchy' Carter was?" When I shrugged he exploded, "He was the goddamn mayor of the ghetto. He was practically born into the Slauson gang, and from that collection of about five thousand angry motherfuckers, he helped create the Slauson Renegades, the baddest niggers in Los Angeles."

"Goddamn!"

"Bunchy spent a few years benefiting from the free college education the government gives poor black kids."

I looked quizzical.

"It's called prison. He majored in self-awareness and freedom as taught by the Black Muslims and Malcolm X. When he got out he found the word according to Huey Newton. Overnight, Bunchy dropped what was left of that fatalistic, goin' nowhere 'cept to hell ghetto gang shit and became a motherfuckin' revolutionary."

"I imagine that's how a lot of black men get involved with the Panthers." I pulled out two Cokes I had in a cooler and handed him one. I was over my macrobiotic phase.

"Incredible insight, motherfucker. I'd say over a thousand gang-bangers and OGs joined the Panthers, especially after Bunchy became the boss man."

"OGs?"

"Original Gangsters, the cats that lived long enough to retire from the street. Bunchy and the Panthers told them they were fools for fighting other black gangs, said they were doing the white man's work by killing black men. They gave them discipline and something to be proud of, and now those young brothers can't wait to become soldiers for their cause."

"What's wrong with that?"

"Nothing and everything's wrong with it. It's what's got J. Edgar Hoover's bowels in an uproar. That and the fact the Panthers are collecting guns like Halloween candy."

"I would think you'd be all for me going out there talking the Panthers up."

"You take those films anywhere but my backyard and I'm all for it."

"So this is racial?"

"Only thing racial is that a brother would know what I'm driving at." He sighed and shook his head. "Hicks, I'm trying to keep you from getting killed, you dumb fuck. You do know about Bunchy and Huggins getting blown away?"

"Sure, by some black FBI agents who…"

"Maybe FBI," he interrupted, "but for sure they were members of the US Organization that's selling Back to Africa like we still slaves speaking Swahili." He shook his head in disgust and drained half the can. "And guess where most of the recruits for US come from?" When I looked blank, he said, "The other black gangs: the Gladiators and the Businessmen. You're stepping into some serious gang shit, a Watts civil war." He saw my surprise and added, "It's like you've gone into downtown Saigon showing movies saying, 'Aren't those Viet Cong wonderful.'"

I argued that it couldn't be that bad and, besides, how could we say no to black groups who wanted to see the films? "But I appreciate you telling me what's going on behind the scenes." I could see that Stanley wished he hadn't brought it up.

"'Appreciate,'" he repeated with a sneer. "I'll tell you something. It doesn't surprise me that white folks don't really understand what it's like to be black, but what blows my mind is that you really don't 'appreciate' what it means to be white." He laughed as if to himself and muttered, "Fuck me for trying to save your dumb, polite, well-meaning ass."

"Look," I insisted, "I can't stand by painting pictures anymore. Things are too corrupt, too fucked up to do nothing. People have to organize and change how things are run and who's running it. That's what a white guy can do."

Stanley eyed me coldly. "Tell me something, what do you hate?"

That stopped me. After a moment I said, "I hate exploitation, inequality, prejudice: all sorts of shit."

"You know what I hate?"

I shook my head.

"I hate the crew-cut DA that put my drug-addicted, prostitute cousin in jail for shoplifting diapers for her baby. I hate the white world that could kill a peace-loving black man like Reverend King, 'cause it shows how much easier it is for them to kill any other kind of nigger. And I hate that most white boys neither hate nor love anything enough to die for it unless the goddamn government tells them to."

"I don't hate or love enough," I repeated softly, turning it over, questioning it.

Stanley looked out the windshield at the darkening sky as a siren wailed past in the distance. He turned to me with sad, old eyes. "Yeah, that's how messed up it is." He rubbed his face. "If it makes you feel any better, it's not natural for me." He hesitated, "Maybe that's why I pick up on it so easily in you. Difference is, I got taught to hate real early."

"Taught?"

"I was about four when my father first told me what happened to his grandpa down in Georgia over a hundred years ago. And the stories were just stories until I was six and some white boy let me know I was a dirty nigger. I was so shocked I didn't do shit. But the next time I was ready, and I turned his fat, freckled nose into a river of blood." He stared off at an angle into the past, and then snapped back. "And you better believe there's a clear line from those stories to us brothers burning down these goddamn urban slave quarters here in the North."

"No shit," I agreed. After a moment I asked, "So what do we do?"

"Damned if I know." He laughed and belched. Serious again, he said, "I do know I got fewer choices than a white boy, but more than those Panther recruits. And choice makes things complicated." He opened the sliding door. "You're okay, Hicks. You gave a real boost to my father, and I'll always owe you for that." He paused, then added, "But you probably won't see me again."

He stepped out and slammed the door shut. I hurried to get out to ask him why or at least give him a hug, but he'd disappeared.

I got behind the wheel and sat in the dark, stunned and confused. I didn't know what to make of his dramatic exit, but I did think he saw things too much from the racial angle. Still, it made me wonder when the first time was that I'd "appreciated" that I was white. It came to me like a little home movie playing behind my eyes: I was seven years old, in the middle of a small mob of second graders running out to recess. Though it was never talked about, there was a near equal mix of white, Mexican, and Indian kids along with a few blacks at school. There was already a disorderly line for the big slide on the playground. With my friend Lewis, I cut in front of numerous others. I turned around giggling at how clever we were and was suddenly locked eye to eye with June, a tall, somber Indian girl staring at me with a coldness that froze the smile on my face. I instantly sensed that my actions had a weight and significance that went far beyond bad manners. I had done something because I could get away with it. My ease and privilege in making the assumption that I could bend the rules and all the pain and anger it caused were there in the glimmering black pools of my classmate's eyes. June was an Indian and I was suddenly white and we'd recreated history on the spot, a history I was only slightly aware of from cowboy-and-Indian serials I'd seen at the Saturday matinees.

I mumbled an apology, knowing that what I had done was rude even if it wasn't all that unusual. Lewis, oblivious to what had transpired, pulled me to the ladder, and up I went with June still smoldering behind me.

The memory dissipated and was replaced by one from eighth grade, one that put my whiteness in a whole other light. As improbable as it sounds, this was a period when I felt more Mexican than anything else. My mother had moved back to Palm Springs, and I had returned to public school after spending seventh grade in Catholic school. I'd barely seen some of my old friends for over a year. I was sitting alone at a lunch table. Suddenly I was surrounded by five white boys, all friends of mine in the past and all apparently mad at me. "Why don't you like hanging out with us anymore? Do you think you're better or what?" Roger demanded.

"Yeah," Bobby chimed in through his braces. "How come you're always messing around with Dagaberto and Moe and those other Mexican guys?"

I was speechless. It was like I'd done something to put them down. Then I realized with surprise that it was true; I was more comfortable hanging with Dag, Moe, and Zooky. I couldn't say it out loud without hurting their feelings, but I also couldn't figure out why they were pissed off. The truth was that they considered themselves better than the Mexican kids. They, and I, were in the college-bound classes where other races were rarely seen. They were confused and threatened that I would voluntarily step lower in the unspoken pecking order. They didn't invent this institutional racism, but they benefitted from it and demanded I support it. I was dumbfounded. I was nowhere near being able to explain why, but it was true that I was inadvertently challenging the system.

When my wits returned, I broke the tension by pointing out that I lived half-time in my stepdad's house, which was just across the street from the reservation, the part of town where a lot of the Indian and Mexican families lived, so it was natural for me to play with those guys after school and on weekends. "It doesn't mean I don't like you guys; it's just how it worked out."

Somewhat satisfied, they sat down to eat with me.

I continued being a guy who had friends in all the various social and racial groups in Junior High. Sitting in my van in the dark, I realized my allegiance to my original circle of white friends had been shattered when my family fell apart. Not that I would have said it like this, but I didn't know who I was: My mom had left, my dad was a basket case, and it seemed like God had abandoned me as well. But we had a Mexican housekeeper whom I loved. When my mom moved out, Emily Romero and her daughter, Helen, two years older than me, moved in full time to live with my dad and me. Over time it was as if I had a Mexican mom and sister. We made a family. When my mom moved back to marry Paul two years later, it seemed natural to become close to those kids near Paul's house. It wasn't until I left Palm Springs for college that I thought of that period following the divorce as my years of being Mexican.

I began to drive. My old neighborhood was only ten minutes away. I drove by the Zamboanga Cafe, a Filipino place where Mike and I had written several scenes for our movie. I made my way past MacArthur Park to Rampart Street and Tommy's, home of a chiliburger that was so good it was immoral and therefore impossible to resist. As usual there were over a dozen people in line. It was always a gas to talk with the cross section of LA who knew about this jewel. But I decided I really wanted to hit my favorite Mexican restaurant on Hoover. Its bright florescence fell on a racially mixed crowd of diners, just like at the rest of the places. It seemed to me that people weren't divided up by race as much as by how much money they had. Because I had enough money to live without working for a few more years, I wasn't working class. I was middle class, which could mean many things. I was white with Mexican tendencies and, according to Stanley, I didn't hate enough to really commit. I felt pushed and pulled from different directions: not enough of one thing, too much of another. I sat down and ate a couple of enchiladas. They weren't nearly as good as Emily's, but they reminded me of my home and family—or at least one of them.

12

VENICE

Most members of the nascent Los Angeles Newsreel lived on the west side of Los Angeles. A flood of requests for films and speakers meant we needed to quickly open an office to run our burgeoning distribution. The obvious choice was funky, cheap Venice, which became a destination for vacationers when it was carved out of the wetlands of the Pacific Ocean at the beginning of the 20th century. It soon fell into shabby neglect, until its reputation was revived somewhat in the 1950s by beatniks and others attracted to its low-rent charm. It carried an aura of casual danger throughout the 60s as home to artists, drugs, bikers, the V13 gang, and Oakwood, its own black and brown ghetto. Main Street had its dusty second-hand stores as it crossed over into Santa Monica, where you could find Olivia's Cafe selling a soul-food chicken dinner for $2.79. An ocean breeze added clean air to a small-town atmosphere that mocked the smoggy metropolis with no center to the east. Venice was low class, working class, and genetically anti-establishment. In other words, it was made for radicals.

Mike found a cottage behind a creaky house with its paint worn off but protected, if not held up, by a profusion of morning glories, wisteria, and bougainvillea. It was owned by Mr. Pettit, a surly old Scotsman and his golden-eyed hound growling at the end of a long, perilously thin chain. When Mike told me that a shack on the grounds, no bigger than twenty-by-twenty feet, was available for fifty bucks a month, I grabbed it. We were across the street from the Fox Venice, the only movie theater for several miles. Its vast second floor was the headquarters for my rock-and-roll/visual artist friends running the Single Wing Turquoise Bird light show along with a variety of other filmmakers of the culturally radical bent, in contrast to the politicos in Newsreel.

The dozen or so who made up the core of Los Angeles Newsreel were a fervent, intense lot. Three of them—serious Jonathan Aurthur, pregnant Judy Belsito, and thoughtful Ron Abrams—reminded me of Jerry, Mary's friend in Indiana: political theoreticians who could explain nearly everything with the help of Marx, Engels, Lenin, Mao, or someone else I'd yet to study. Others, like Judy's husband Peter Belsito, Barbara Rose, and Tim Hinkle had thoughtful but less theory-based explanations for the contradictions that plagued our society. There was usually some discussion hanging in the air ready to be rehashed if one wanted to have a go, like, "Is democracy simply a ploy by the very rich to hide their control of America behind the illusion of freedom and choice?" If you said yes to that—and eventually we all did—it was difficult not to begin conjuring up some sort of workers' control of the state. But what we were organizing for was very much a vision in progress. Some worked full time, but others were students with flexible schedules. Along with volunteers who often showed up, we began to meet every Saturday to organize the office, coordinate the screenings, and discuss the issues that had come up when we went out with the films. The general goals were to deepen and extend the anti-war movement beyond a student base and to promote the necessity for a radical change to our soulless, sold-out government.

We were about two months into this when I told my new cohorts that a black friend had warned me about going out with the Panther film. Most seemed to believe that a reactionary black organization, even one propped up by the FBI, would not dare to attack white radicals like us. There was an assumption that we weren't vulnerable to the extremes of the governmental crackdown that had already been felt by the Panthers in both LA and Oakland. Nobody was proud of the fact that some of our protection was racial, that "white privilege" was at play, but there was more to it. Barbara believed the biggest difference was that we weren't armed with guns. We carried films and projectors; we carried ideas and news. Sometimes we carried cameras. We figured the government didn't like us, but in the USA, so far, they weren't fighting ideas with guns, even though that was basically what was happening in Vietnam. Theoretically, our "free speech" was still protected by the Constitution. Of course, as Judy pointed out, theoretically the Panthers' right to carry guns was protected as well, but that wasn't stopping the police from killing and harassing them. At this point, Jonathan jumped in with a short lecture: "Race is secondary to class. Marx made it clear that the goals and needs of the capitalist class are in contradiction, in direct opposition, to those of the working class. It may become more dangerous, but anything we can do to expose and heighten this inherent conflict will bring about the revolution and the inevitable triumph of socialism."

Bill Floyd, a New York Newsreel member who'd come out to help us get going, said in a mocking professorial tone, "'The contradictions are being heightened,' as our SDS brothers would say." His eyes gleamed; he'd already declared he was impatient for the real revolution to begin. He'd gotten his head cracked while filming the police taking back the buildings at Columbia University. "Being white won't protect our asses if we're attacking private property. But the thing is, people are challenging power and property all over the fucking country. Righteous action is happening, man, and we've got to tell the world."

As we began to get to know the LA Panthers, including the new Minister of Education Masai Hewitt and Minister of Defense Geronimo Pratt, they made it clear what everyone's role was: While their current efforts were focused on the black community, they were the vanguard of a multiracial revolution of the working class and the lumpenproletariat. Even though most of their energies were going into benign, socialist-style community programs like providing a free breakfast for the local children, the Los Angeles police were making life difficult for them daily. The Panthers stood for radical and, perhaps, violent change, and that's why they were taking the most heat. We expressed our common cause and support by suggesting that we might make a film, which the Panthers could use for organizing, about the recent assassinations and the role of the Panthers in contrast to the capitalist-oriented Black Nationalist movement. Although the widows of John Huggins and Bunchy Carter were wary of white radicals handling any aspect of their respective husbands' image and legacy, the party agreed to cooperate. But there was no question that we had to finance it.

As Stanley had intimated, the Panthers got some support from their communities. However, big bucks were obtained from squeezing wealthy liberals in the New York and Hollywood entertainment industry. Through inspiration and guilt-tripping, they had raised a lot of money and, rumor had it, built up quite an arsenal of weapons to arm a large underground guerilla force. Nonetheless, cash was in short supply, and Panthers were having trouble keeping their free programs going.

Undeterred, LA Newsreel collectively began to consider what this film might look like. At the same time, we had to deal with the fact that there were other documentaries that the group wanted to make, including an exposé of the gentrification of Venice and another on feminism. It took time for our new group to figure out even how to decide, much less what we were going to do. There was filmmaking experience in the group, but we had limited man/woman power and very limited finances. We had no one with deep pockets, no wealthy Hollywood filmmaker had come forward to support our work, nor had we gone to any. We had shown films at gatherings at the homes of wealthy liberals and debated the issues, but we took no more than rental fees.

The one concrete advantage Newsreel had over purely political organizations was its films. We could show what revolutionary change looked like and give a face to the worst social problems and the most dramatic and radical of solutions. We figured we could combine a few films with a dynamite speaker and raise some serious cash. Someone in our group had contact with Professor Herbert Marcuse, a well-known Marxist theoretician at the University of California in San Diego. Plans were begun for a fundraiser in May with Professor Marcuse slated to speak.

Getting politicized didn't mean that sex was forgotten. In ways few had foreseen—certainly men hadn't—the sexual was political as more and more women demanded equality and new roles. I had shared my bed and revolutionary fervor with several women, ranging from an Asian filmmaker to an ex-Vegas showgirl with two kids. But none of the women involved in Newsreel had sparked my interest until Stephanie Waxman strode into a Saturday meeting. Tall with long black hair, slender yet wonderfully busty, her dark eyes smiled as we met and my mind was definitely not on politics. I decided Newsreel needed to run down the coast to distribute flyers advertising our fundraiser and asked for a helper. Stephanie volunteered, and off we went to spread the word at head shops and bookstores from Venice to Laguna Beach.

I quickly discovered much in common with Stephanie. Like me, she was a painter who was also interested in film. But there were major differences too. Her parents were both actors, and her dad had been blacklisted during the McCarthy era. As a "red diaper baby," she'd been nursed on radical ideas. While I was more up-to-date with the issues, she was more politically seasoned. Our conversation moved back and forth from art to politics to poignant personal history, all of it sprinkled with flirtatious humor. It was a day of exquisite foreplay that was suddenly brought to a halt as we drove back at sunset into LA. Until then, Stephanie had omitted telling me that, although she was thinking of leaving him, she was living with someone.

It wasn't easy, but I quickly sobered up from the cocktail of erotic possibilities that we'd been mixing. I liked that she was *"experienced,"* as Jimi Hendrix sang. I wanted that in a woman. I was convinced that my parents' marriage was doomed by their being virgins when they got married and not being allowed to practice birth control. Nonetheless, I told Stephanie I didn't want to treat whatever we might have together as a secret fling. The new seriousness I felt about myself in the world extended into all aspects of my life. I was tired of playing around. I wanted to commit myself more seriously to whatever I did. So we didn't go to my place. Instead, I dropped her off and urged her to call me as soon as she was free. I could tell she was rather shocked but impressed. I added that I was driving to Washington, D.C., for the first national Newsreel gathering, and I'd be back in a month.

※

Ron had to get his station wagon back to the East Coast but didn't have time to drive it. Bill Woods was one of those who clustered around Newsreel and the Fox Venice, getting involved as the mood struck. He volunteered to share the drive to D.C. with me. From there he said he'd hitch to his home in Cooperstown, New York, also the home of the Baseball Hall of Fame and the source of his nickname: Baseball Billy.

I'd returned to a mostly macrobiotic diet, and both Billy and I had been living light and clean: no drugs and no alcohol for months. We baked wheat bread in coffee cans for our trip. Along with a couple of gallon wine jugs filled with water, we figured we wouldn't have to stop except for gas and piss stops until Albuquerque. Baseball Billy proved to be full of stories. At least some of them were completely true. He was a self-sufficient, nomadic kid who seemed older than his twenty years. We sailed right through New Mexico, and after almost twenty-four hours, we got off the interstate and slept out under the stars.

The next morning we found a cafe in Clinton, Oklahoma, where we washed up and had breakfast. As we pulled out of town, we came across two young hitchhikers. Their hair was medium length, about as long as someone who was at the beginning of daring to be different. I looked at Billy and he shrugged, "Do unto others..." and we let them into the backseat of Ron's station wagon. They turned out to be brothers: Buzz, seventeen, and Wally, nineteen, trying to get home to St. Louis.

After a few minutes of silence, the older one evidently figured that my very long hair and beard made me safe to open up to, and started to tell their story. "Damn truck driver kicked us out in the middle of the night when this idiot," and here he punched the younger one, "told him I was thinking of going to Canada."

"Wally!" the kid yelped, rubbing his arm and looking guilty. "I thought he was cool after he went on and on for a hundred miles on how much he liked the Cardinals and thought Stan Musial was the best player ever, black or white. He said he wanted to buy my baseball card collection."

Billy laughed the loudest. "I know baseball fanatics, and they are no fans of peace. I learned the hard way that there are two national pastimes in this country: baseball and war."

"Why are you guys hitching around?" I asked.

"Our aunt is in medical school in Berkeley," Wally began.

"She's a pacifist," Buzz interrupted, "the complete opposite of our mom."

"...and she always told me she would help me if I wanted to get out of the draft, so three days ago I took off and Dumbo here decided to come along."

"It's not like I was going to miss anything at my stupid high school," Buzz added.

"When we got to Denver, I called Aunt Jeanette to tell her we were coming. She told me that my mom had already figured out where we were going. My mom had called Jeanette and told her she'd never talk to her again if Jeanette helped me avoid the damn war."

Buzz jumped in, "Aunt Jeanette told us that she was taking care of hundreds of people the cops had beat up at something called 'People's Park' in Berkeley. They shot them with shotguns and tear-gassed them real bad."

"My aunt said we had to go back and that she'd send me some people to contact about going to Canada…"

"…if we promised not to tell Mom."

"Sounds like a lot families these days," Billy murmured.

The hours went quickly with this sibling sideshow for entertainment. Late that afternoon we pulled into a gas station a few miles before St. Louis to allow the boys to contribute to the gas budget. We almost didn't make it out of there.

The three of them had gone to the head while the attendant filled the tank and took some of the bugs off the windshield. When he finished I pulled to the side of the station so I wouldn't block the pumps while I took a piss. I started to get out when I noticed a black car creeping around the back of the station. Something about it screamed "unmarked police car." Sure enough, a big guy in plain clothes with a graying crew cut stepped out and approached me flashing a badge. Buzz came back at the same time.

"What're you boys planning on doing, robbing this place?"

"We're just passing through," I replied steadily. Wally approached, combing out his hair.

The cop looked at us scornfully. "We don't like long-hair assholes around here, especially since your friends created so much trouble for real Americans in Chicago last summer."

"We just needed some gas and to take a piss," I explained.

Buzz decided he had something to add. "People have a right to protest the war, don't they?" he asked innocently like he was in a civics class.

"Not if you're some goddamn coward who's not man enough to fight!" the cop erupted and started swearing at him. I had to pee real bad and hurried off to the bathroom so we could split.

When I came back the sheriff, or whatever he was, was haranguing the brothers with his take on the domino theory and how they were playing into the hands of "the goddamn commies." I slid into the driver's seat. Billy wasn't in sight. Just then a regular cop car raced in and squealed to a stop. A pimply-faced uniformed guy jumped out and ran over to his boss. The sheriff gave him a few orders and, puffed up like a rooster, returned to lambasting the boys. The rookie, hand resting on his gun, hurried over to me and announced he was going to search the car for "contraband." Without even asking for an ID, he moved around to the passenger side where the door was open and stuck his head in. "What kind of good shit am I going to find in here?" he asked. He picked out one of Billy's hand-rolled cigarette butts from the ashtray and smiled. "Mary Jane, why isn't that surprising?"

"Smell it. It's tobacco. My buddy rolls his own."

He smelled it and frowned. Evidently he knew the difference. He spied a San Antonio wine jug under Billy's sweater on the floor. "Well, drinking and driving, I see. That'll do for some jail time."

"Just water," I said, trying to stay calm. "Go ahead, smell that too."

He did, screwed the top back on, and tossed it on the front seat, cursing under his breath. He went to the rear door on the passenger side and tried to open it. When it wouldn't budge, he commanded me to unlock it.

"It's broken," I said, "I can't."

"Open this goddamn door!" he shouted and started yanking on the handle with both hands.

"It's okay with me if you want to open it, but I can't. It's broken."

Suddenly he whipped out his pistol, leaned into the car from the front passenger side, and held it inches from my temple. "Open up that goddamn door," he swore menacingly.

I turned and saw a punk .22 pistol. A strange stillness descended upon me. What a ridiculous, candy-assed way to go, I thought. I looked into the pinpoint eyes of the sweaty, pockmarked face of my would-be executor and answered with all the sincerity I could muster, "You are welcome to open it, Officer, but I can't. I know it's frustrating, but it's broken."

The rookie looked at his gun as if he were surprised to see it and awkwardly backed out as he holstered it. Out of the corner of my eye, I noticed Billy come around the corner from the market and stop short. For the first time, I was scared. If he ran, and I felt sure he was considering it, the cops would have a whole new reason to be suspicious. I called to him and waved him over. Like a skittish cat, he walked around the deputy and got in.

The sheriff was approaching with the brothers. He eyed me with disdain. "You get these two pussy bastards out of my sight now!" As the boys got into the back, he told them, "And you young punks better watch out what kind of troublemakers you accept rides from."

The sheriff stood next to the car. "Now, all you sons-a-bitches get outta my sight."

"We're going," I said as I turned on the engine. I looked over my left shoulder to see if I could back up only to notice Buzz flash the sheriff the peace sign, sincerity plastered all over his face.

"Stop, goddamn it!" he roared, yanked open the rear door, and pulled the kid out of the car without his feet touching the ground. The sheriff, about six feet of overfed Midwestern beef, shook the innocence out of that boy until he was about to come apart. Then he flung him back in the car and gasped noisily, "I lost too many friends in that goddamn jungle to take this shit." He caught his breath and stuck his face in mine. "You know what we can do with hippie pinkos like you? We take you downtown late at night and push your chickenshit heads through the plate glass of some store. If you survive that, we charge you with robbery and put you away for a long, long time."

I looked at him in total belief. He straightened up and rested his hand on his pistol. "You got thirty seconds to get outta this town or you won't ever leave in one piece."

It was silent in the car for a long time after we roared onto the freeway. Finally, Billy demanded, "What'd you tell that cop about us?"

Wally hemmed and hawed until Buzz answered, "I told him you guys were making revolutionary films."

"Revolutionary?" I asked. "What the hell does that mean?"

Buzz laughed weakly, "That's what he said."

"And?" Billy asked.

"I said I wasn't sure but I thought it was cool."

"Your brother's right," Billy said. "You are an idiot."

We got off the freeway at the exit they wanted in St. Louis. We made them get out at the base of the ramp and said they could walk the rest of the way home. A couple of hours later, we splurged on a cheap motel. A few roaches scurried when Billy pulled back the shower curtain to clean off the grit, but like he said, "As long as it's not a jail cell. I don't ever want to land there again." I was too tired to ask him what he meant.

꩜

We met Ron in D.C. and were soon plunged into the confusion and brotherhood of New Left, radical, counter-cultural political debate. It was soon too much for Billy, and he drifted off to a freeway on-ramp to stick out his thumb. But I loved it. It was clear that Newsreel was a microcosm of the general social and political scene. There were the "good vibe, bad vibe" cultural folks, the "our job is to make the contradictions clear" gradualists, and the "we've got to be ready to go underground" revolutionaries. The result was a fermenting, intoxicating mash of people and ideas that heralded major changes.

After the official conference was over, Ron and I headed up to New York to visit the original Newsreel group. They were, by far, the biggest organization, with over a hundred showing up for meetings. Some were known in the alternative film world, like Robert Kramer, who had recently done a film called *Ice* about white radicals that was akin to the doomed *Little White Whiskers* that Mike and I had attempted. For my money his film didn't overcome the same problems we'd faced: Just what do white radicals envision after the revolution? Nonetheless, he'd finished his film and shown it at festivals and theaters. He was clearly seen as worrisome enough that the FBI was trailing him around, taking pictures of him and his associates whenever possible.

I realized this when I met with Kramer and few others from New York Newsreel in a little pocket park in lower Manhattan. They thought their office might be bugged. As we talked, I saw some photographer positioning the girl he was supposedly taking shots of so that we were always behind her. He could then point his long lens at us while it looked like he was taking shots of her. The New Yorkers seemed blasé about surveillance, but they hadn't had a recent experience like I had with the sheriff. People who looked different and trafficked in radical ideas were being watched. I realized that I was going to have to get used to it.

That night we went to a party in an East Village loft that was jammed with an assortment of New York leftists. Ron was sure one out of ten was an undercover cop. We were talking about different demonstrations with an intense girl, or "woman" as she'd insisted a few minutes earlier.

"As long as you're not blowing up shit, there's not much they can get you for. Just hassle your ass." She exhaled cigarette smoke toward the open skylight. "They jailed me for illegal assembly at one of the demonstrations, but we were out in a few hours." She leaned over to scratch her unshaved leg. Her blouse fell open, exposing her breasts. "It's all Hoover's bullshit." She glanced up to see if I was checking her out, but I'd already shifted my gaze, oddly unmoved. She added, "He thinks he can stop this organic uprising of the people with that shit." She shifted gears. "So, I hear you guys are doing a doc in color. That's so bourgeois."

I'd heard this dumb critique about five times already and said, "We're thinking about changing our name to Hollywood Newsreel. We've already got a Cadillac convertible to take us to screenings." To her credit, she smiled.

Ron responded more defensively. "It's pretty hard to show smog in black and white. Anyway, it's just one idea of many we're considering." He looked at her and seemed to think she was cute. He changed his tone and added, "We've also been thinking about making one on the women's movement." With that, they were off into a passionate discussion about feminism that ended at her place.

Myself, I wasn't driven to score. Instead, I kept wondering if I was going to hear from Stephanie when I got back to LA. The next day, several members from San Francisco Newsreel and I drove back nonstop. True to the enthusiasm of our first meeting, Stephanie soon called to announce she was single once again and would love to see me. While we quickly consummated our lengthy flirtation and began to get to know one another in earnest, I was equally drawn in by my new life as a radical filmmaker, distributor, and political organizer. It was an added bonus that Stephanie was interested in being a part of that effort as well.

Bill Floyd and I began weekly screenings at the Black Panther office as part of the intensive educational barrage that greeted a seemingly endless stream of new recruits. At every screening there were fifty or sixty mostly young black men and women seriously attending to the films and lectures. They may have been high school dropouts or Vietnam vets, but all were expected to memorize the Panther ten-point program, study Mao's Little Red Book and other literature, and represent the Party to the community with respect and maturity. Most of their recruits were unemployed or underemployed: nurses' aides, maintenance men, domestics, cooks, street hustlers, gangbangers, and welfare mothers along with pimps, prostitutes, thieves, and others who lived outside the law. Like the workers in 1917 Russia, and the peasants in 1949 China, this was the part of America most motivated to join a revolution. It sure looked like that to me. Furthermore, as Bill reminded me, we were seeing only the part of the Party that was above ground.

The Panthers were happy to work with us. They were serious about their commitment to a multiracial revolutionary effort. More importantly, in spite of the assassinations at UCLA and continual police harassment, their recruitment was extremely successful. Over a hundred years after slavery was abolished, capitalist America still hadn't delivered equality, and they were pulling together a lot of people ready to fight for a socialist America. The Panthers weren't spouting some dry theory. They were attempting to mold the "vanguard of the revolution," which was getting bigger every day. Stanley's warning that gang hostilities would make working with the Panthers dangerous for white outsiders seemed more and more like paranoia.

That's not to say there weren't cultural differences and occasional clashes. One that took me by surprise was the way that some Black Panthers used the word "pussy." As the feminist movement gained ground, white men were quickly learning that coming onto a woman about "getting some pussy" was a sure way not to get laid. However, among certain Panthers, "pussy power" was revolutionary.

I learned about this from Raymond, a Panther who had recently come down from Oakland. He was into photography and the Party wanted him to learn how to develop photographs to use in their newspaper and elsewhere. They asked me to teach him how to use a darkroom. He was bright, a quick study, and as we worked we developed a casual camaraderie. He'd taken some great pictures of women that got us talking about sex, and it was then I was introduced to the revolutionary notion of "pussy power."

As we waited for the black-and-white images to appear under the moody, red safelight in the darkroom, Raymond explained, "A righteous sister knows that if a righteous Panther brother wants it, the sister got to give it up." When I told him that the women I knew would consider this sexist and disrespectful, he said some of the sisters in LA were like that but that it was different up north. "Sisters know we respect them so much we willing to die for them." He agreed that women were in charge of their own bodies, "same as men," except when it came to supporting the revolution, "same as men." To him, it was both righteous and fair that men and women both give their bodies to the revolution. "Pussy be what a woman gives a brother for putting his life on the line."

"Like a reward for a warrior?" I asked.

"Yeah, and like an obligation for the sister." He went on to suggest that judging blacks for looking at sex differently was racist. It was tense for a moment until we both agreed that whatever our differences, we both dug the sexual revolution.

Near the end of June, Jonathan, the staunchest of Newsreel's Marxists, returned from the SDS conference in Chicago and announced that the Revolutionary Youth Movement (RYM) had taken control of the SDS national office after a fierce debate with other Marxist factions. In fact, RYM itself had split in two. "The old SDS leadership in RYM 1 are pushing violent confrontations with the cops," he said with disdain. "They call themselves Weathermen and think that organizing means getting people hit on the head by a pig."

"But, you gotta admit, that does get someone thinking," Bill said. "It sure radicalized me when I got bashed by the cops at Columbia."

Judy cut in. "Don't you get it? RYM 1 is trying to start a revolution before they have the working class firmly behind them. It's cynical and suicidal!"

"But isn't this what the Panthers are doing?" I asked.

"No," Jonathan insisted. "The material conditions are different. Racism and economic oppression have given black Americans a more advanced stage of revolutionary consciousness, and that's who the Panthers are organizing. But even they aren't starting a guerilla war."

"Not yet," Judy added.

"They're organizing the black nation," Jonathan said. "It's the white radicals' job to raise consciousness among the white working class, not to concoct some revolutionary fantasy involving students with handmade bombs and rocks taking state control."

"But your argument didn't win in Chicago," he was reminded by Stephanie, now an active member. "So where does that leave Newsreel?"

Judy answered, "We and the RYM 11 people are doing the hard work of organizing. It's what those leftwing opportunists and anarchists can't handle. Every day this system does something else to radicalize a few thousand more people. Millions have turned against the system, but most don't know what to do next. So we show films and talk up the need for revolutionary change. In a few weeks up in Oakland, the Panthers are taking the next step by pulling together all the different factions of the movement to form the United Front

Against Fascism. Read this pamphlet by Georgi Dimitrov and you'll understand the historical context."

Bill stood up. "Both this meeting and the revolution are taking too damn long. I'm going to the Brig for some working-class beer and a game of pool, if anybody wants to join me."

Most everyone did.

13

PANTHERS IN OAKLAND

Three towns surrounding the San Francisco Bay gave shape to the forces that came to define the 60s as radical. Taking inspiration from the struggle for civil rights in the American South, the Free Speech Movement blossomed at the University of California at Berkeley. That, in turn, gave impetus to much of the anti-Vietnam War ferment. What became the Cultural Revolution initially came into focus on the streets of San Francisco, across the bay. Simultaneously, if you followed Telegraph Avenue south from Berkeley, you soon crossed into Oakland, California, the home of the Black Panther Party for Self-Defense. This tough working-class port town proved to be fertile ground for a black community that had had enough of putting up with the same ol', same ol'. Evidently something about the San Francisco Bay fomented revolutionary ideas, since all three movements shared the objective of profoundly changing society.

As Judy had announced, the Black Panther Party in Oakland was taking on the job of uniting the many disparate and often feuding radical and progressive groups across the country. For three days in July, we were to come together under the banner of the United Front Against Fascism in order to coordinate our respective battles against a warmongering, racist America. It was a daunting, courageous task, and necessary for the growth of the movement. That may have been the only thing everyone could agree on. As hosts of the gathering, and as the vanguard of the movement, the Panthers were going to run the show, whether one agreed or not.

Stef, Mike, and I had driven up in my van. We knew that Jonathan and Elinor Schiffrin, a veteran of the civil rights movement, were also coming but didn't expect to see them much. They were going to be busy with old friends and political connections. Stef said she would come for the first day, but made it clear that she had come up mostly to visit with friends from her college days in Berkeley.

Over four thousand showed up during the weekend. The first day of the conference was fascinating, if not a little intimidating. The Panthers carefully searched bags and patted down the curious and the radicals of all stripes, as well as the inevitable undercover cops, each time we came into the gigantic Oakland Auditorium. There were Panthers standing along the sides of the auditorium and across the front, below the stage. They were in uniform: black leather jackets, dark glasses, and big Afros. If anyone was armed, it was those guys. It was an impressive show of strength, and a bit scary. Not that I didn't believe that their cause—our cause—was righteous; the movement was splintering and we needed to create a coalition, a united front to coordinate all the different groups who were challenging our government as it calcified into fascism. It was a necessary, bold step for an organization that was out to prove it was the vanguard. We heard from other communist, socialist, and progressive groups, everyone it seemed except for the Trotskyites who were turned away. Regardless of ideology, the speakers tended to go on and on. Mike disappeared early.

Stef decided not to go the second day. In the few months we'd been seeing each other, I found she had far less tolerance for harangues or the abstract nature of political theory and debate than I. I enjoyed arguing ideas and concepts. She found it all fairly irrelevant until they were turned into concrete deeds and actions. Fortunately, it turned me on how practical and down-to-earth she was.

It turned out that the Panthers were practical as well. While others described the world according to Marxist theory, including whether "fascist" was the right word for our government, the Panthers pointed out that police had killed nineteen Panthers in the last year. Violent oppression wasn't an abstraction in the black community: Fascism was real to them. However, the word "fascism" invoked comparison with the Nazis and Mussolini. While the U.S. wasn't yet fascist to that extent, it was clear that the government was illegally targeting certain parts of the population, beginning with the Panthers.

I was reminded that the nature of this problem had been immortalized in the famous poem by German pastor Martin Niemöller:

> First they came for the Communists,
> and I didn't speak out because I wasn't a Communist.
> Then they came for the Trade Unionists,
> and I didn't speak out because I wasn't a Trade Unionist.
> Then they came for the Jews,
> and I didn't speak out because I wasn't a Jew.
> Then they came for me,
> and there was no one left to speak for me.

Those of us who had gathered at the Panthers' invitation for the weekend were certainly speaking out. And, true to the spirit of the Bay area, there were other ways of speaking out that were being celebrated that same weekend.

I met up with Stef at a party Saturday night and soon found myself talking with participants of numerous radical actions including the Free Speech Movement in '64. I shared a joint with FJ, an old friend of Stef's who was as close to being a leader as was allowed in Berkeley's anti-authoritarian atmosphere. He was a graduate school dropout and one of the Oakland 7. Everyone was celebrating their acquittals on charges of conspiracy during Stop the Draft Week in Oakland back in 1967. They had taken concrete action, attempting to block buses filled with draftees heading for the Army induction center. Actions like this had inspired thousands of kids to burn their draft cards and get out of the country.

"Screw the courts," he said in a billow of smoke. "I mean, I'm relieved to be acquitted, but we don't accept the political authority of this government. They can bust us but they cannot make us obey."

"I've been listening to a lot of Marxists this weekend. Do you consider yourself one?" I asked, taking the joint he offered.

"I doubt they'd have me—I'm sure the Leninists wouldn't." He laughed, "I'm in the political outlaw party, anarchist wing." Looking around the packed room, he added, "Like most everyone here."

A curly-headed guy who'd been sharing the joint leaned in and pointed to his forehead. "The mind may be a theorist, but the rest is pure anarchist." He nodded sagely and began dancing and weaving through the crowd.

"People have really been turned on by People's Park," FJ said.

"Even though it's been shut down?" I asked.

"Did you ever see what we built?" he asked. I shook my head. "It was beautiful, man. In three weeks the whole community, young and old of all political persuasions and colors, turned an ugly dirt lot into a thing of beauty and hope: flowers, trees, grass, and free speech. The university wasn't using the land, so we took it back for the common good, like it was before they ripped it off from the Costanoan Indians hundreds of years ago. It was inspirational. We washed the blood of colonialism off the land," he ended with dramatic flair.

"And they covered it with our blood," a young kid who'd been listening added. "The Highway Patrol and the Berkeley fuzz came in one morning and bulldozed part of the park and put a fence around it. Thousands of us confronted them, and the pigs attacked us with nightsticks and shotguns. We were just throwing dirt clods and bottles and shit." He pulled his shirt up and showed me three small circular scars on his back. "Buckshot," he said. "Bastards killed one guy and messed up hundreds more."

"I'm glad you made it," I said.

He was still too young for much of a beard, but his eyes gleamed. "It's either me or this fucked-up system. One of us isn't going to make it." He gave the clenched fist power salute to us and left.

"Sounds like Chicago last summer," I said to FJ.

"And then some," he responded. "We weren't looking for a fight… necessarily. This wasn't about Vietnam or civil rights. This was everyday Americans challenging private property, and Governor Reagan showed us what the state and corporate America thought of that."

"That's some heavy shit," I said. "The contradictions are being seriously tightened."

"You think it's going to take more than a student movement?" he asked evenly.

"I guess I do. It's why I'm up here at the Panther Conference. What about you?"

"It's really, really hard to give up that fantasy," he sighed, "but it's getting even harder to hold onto it, even with good kids like Randy getting drawn in." He sat back. "Right now I'm enjoying the fact that I'm not going to jail for trying to stop a few guys from being drafted." He took a slug of beer. "So, an anti-fascist conference. That sounds like a kick."

"Political theory is… well, wake me when the revolution starts," I laughed.

"Well, you're in interesting company. Stalin, Churchill, and Roosevelt formed the first united front against fascism to defeat Hitler. Goes to show you that communists and capitalists can be friends if need be."

"Not now. Not according to the SDS guy who spoke," I said.

Stef and two girlfriends emerged through the dancers, and she plopped down on my lap in high spirits. "Jane and Regina are taking me to a dance concert tomorrow night, so you're on your own."

"You go have fun," I said. "I'll start the revolution."

"Stephanie," FJ said, "seems like you have become more serious in your choice of men."

"You mean she's had other boyfriends?" I asked with mock surprise.

Stef jumped off and pulled me up to dance to a serious boogie laid down by the Paul Butterfield Blues Band.

I made it back to the Panthers the next morning, but the speakers didn't have much new to add. Mike had disappeared during most of the weekend to hang out with an old girlfriend. That afternoon he returned to the conference to convince me to join him at the bar. My growing sense of urgency and moral responsibility, along with the strengthening and clarifying of my own political will, made it hard to leave early, even if only by an hour or two. But after nearly three days of political analysis, cheerleading, and pontification from an endless array of speakers, I broke loose.

We settled into a dark, air-conditioned bar in the black part of town. A Nina Simone song curled seductively from the jukebox. It was 6:00 p.m., Sunday, July 20, 1969. I was sipping the first of what I trusted would be many beers. Mike balanced on his stool with a serene smile, eyes closed. He was smiling because I'd just admitted to him that I wanted to split earlier, but it felt like I would be running out of church: liberating, but a political sacrilege. He understood that; he was recovering from Catholicism too, but he had yet to see the wisdom or inevitability of the Marxist analysis.

"Willow Weep for Me" ended and Mike's smile disappeared. "Man, the Panthers are talking up this multiracial stuff, but one thing I know for sure; if black people are the ones getting shot at, they sure as hell aren't going to give up that vanguard spot once good ol' socialism comes around. Like, 'Hey, Mr. Whitey, now that we got control, would you help us run this thing?' No way, no fucking way. And from what I've seen this weekend, having blacks in control wouldn't lead to a much better situation than we got now. I think a President Huey Newton or General Eldridge Cleaver could be just as scary as fucking Nixon, Governor Reagan, and General Westmoreland."

"That's pure racism, to think blacks couldn't run the country."

"That's not what I'm saying. I'm saying that, judging by how they ran this convention, if these guys who happen to be black were in control of the Socialist States of America, it would be a police state. You can't tell me you didn't feel intimidated, and that's exactly what they wanted us to feel."

"Okay, there's a militaristic, tough-guy edge, but that's because we are up against the strongest military in the world. That's why they patted us down for weapons."

"Bull! That same rationale ended up with Stalin killing everybody who talked back in Russia. The whole conference was to show that they were in control and wouldn't take shit from cops or white radicals. You saw them kick out those idiots from the Progressive Labor Party, and then they had some Marxist parrot up there mimicking their position that no one who's a capitalist or a Democrat could possibly be progressive. He reminded me of a white Uncle Tom."

"I still say you're being racist."

"They could be any race. I'm saying that the political solution they are fighting for is a dictatorship like the other communist countries have, and from all appearances, they are practicing for it right here."

"Now you're being paranoid."

"I wish." He drained the bottle. "I'm going to call a non-conference entitled 'The Disorganized but Omnipresent Front Against All Government'...DOFAAG!" He ordered us another round and was soon absorbed in drawing a quick but accurate portrait of the waitress on a cocktail napkin.

Mike and I were mirror images of one another. He was an anarchist in spirit and philosophy, but not in his art. For all the disorganization and disorder that his politics indicated, he was a consummate draughtsman. On a piece of paper, he was as orderly and controlled as a Soviet courtroom even if the results were more impressive. He chose odd subjects, but he could recreate reality down to the shadow of an eyelash. I was the reverse. My paintings tended to be bold, anarchistic expressions of passion and color, but my politics were beginning to reflect the predictability of my old religious beliefs: dogmatic, severe, and righteous. Where I was right, Mike was left, and vice versa. It may have been the beers, but I found all this very funny and began to laugh. Mike had no idea why, but he didn't need one and joined in with gusto.

A photo of Teddy Kennedy appeared on the TV behind the bar, and I asked the bartender to turn it up. The newscaster was wrapping up a segment about a woman being drowned in an auto accident in some place called Chappaquiddick. Then he announced they were going to live coverage of the lunar module *Eagle* as it landed on the surface of the moon. I hadn't told Mike, but this was the main reason I let him talk me into leaving the conference early.

As the lunar module was slowly descending to the moon's surface, the bar filled up. Mike brought our conversation back to racism: "I grew up around rednecks in Akron. Those cats were racist to the core. But the funny thing is, if you talked to them after several beers, one reason those honky bigots held such nasty, harsh opinions of blacks was the result of a weird kind of empathy."

"Empathy?" I nearly choked on my beer nuts.

"Exactly. It wasn't always conscious, but at some level they knew that if they had been treated as badly as blacks were, they'd go ballistic. They'd be like a Hells Angel with a righteous cause and go off on anyone who was in any way responsible for their pain."

"So, let me get this right. A racist is a white guy who's actually empathetic to black people being screwed over."

"Correctamundo!"

"So why does he hate blacks?"

"Because he knows how righteously angry blacks are and he's scared. He can't join 'em. He can't help 'em. So, consciously he hates 'em, but unconsciously he's afraid of them. Matter of fact, this isn't limited to obvious racists. I think it's true of about any American who isn't black." He looked supremely satisfied. "Tell me I'm wrong."

"Well, you're making an interesting case that white America has a strong moral, empathic center. But if that were true, it seems to me that racism—to say nothing of slavery— would have been knocked out much earlier."

"Well, shit, Lone Ranger, if Americans truly acted on their moral principles of fairness and equality, of course it would be a very different place." He pointed to the TV and we watched as the silhouette of a figure emerged from the module in faded black-and-white. "For one thing, that cat in the funny suit might be Navajo or black or, heaven forbid, a lesbian."

I glanced at my watch. It was almost 8:00 p.m. Astronaut Neil Armstrong was coming down a ladder, and for several minutes the whole bar was silent, mesmerized by the stark audacity of a man becoming part of the moonscape. When he stepped off, we heard through the static, "That's one small step for man, one giant leap for mankind." Some patrons cheered. An elderly black man next to me downed his shot of whiskey, finished his beer, and shakily pushed off his stool. He looked at me through rheumy, bloodshot eyes, straightened up, and declared that now they could use his taxes to create decent jobs for poor blacks. Using his cane for balance, he exited a celebration he wanted no part of. Nonetheless, like me, he'd wanted to see the first man on the moon.

Buzz Aldrin joined Neil Armstrong, and for the next hour they bounced around the Sea of Tranquility like four-year-olds on a trampoline. In spite of all the contradictory political implications, I felt like another little kid at the party, overcome with a joyful giddiness and sense of wonder. Humans had disconnected from the earth and made it to the moon. I couldn't help but celebrate this astounding accomplishment, but I soon began to feel disconnected too. The same country that sent a rocket to the moon sent B-52s to drop bombs on North Vietnam and Laos. To the United Front Against Fascism and the old guy at the bar, the only thing the race to the moon meant was less money for the poor and oppressed. The lunar landing underscored the fact that we were in the midst of a lunacy, something pretty well agreed upon by all Americans. Maybe the only thing.

14

NEWSREEL

I'd been raised to believe that there was an All-Powerful, All-Seeing God, with whom the Catholic Church had a special relationship. This paralleled the general assumption—which is a lot like a belief—that we lived under the greatest political system devised by humans: Democratically elected leaders were kept in line by spreading out the power between the Presidency, the Congress, and the Supreme Court—checks and balances. The political and the religious were intertwined and, in case anyone had other ideas, "under God" was added right after "one nation" to the Pledge of Allegiance when I was twelve years old. My politics and my religion seemed to walk hand in hand, except that around the same time and no matter how often I implored him, God couldn't even keep my parents living in the same house. I began to see gaping holes in the priests' argument, and once sexual fever had me in its grip, I was headed out of the Church.

A little over a decade later, a similar thing had happened to my political faith. What was the point of being able to vote if the good guys were killed, the remaining leaders lied in order to get elected, and the President did what he wanted in spite of Congress and the courts? Elections and the highly touted democratic process were a farce. Despite constant claims to the contrary, there wasn't a choice between our democracy and a dictatorship; there was our dictatorship of the wealthy wizards hiding behind the curtain of democracy and other dictatorial systems. I was smack up against the stark choice articulated by Eldridge Cleaver, the exiled Minister of Information of the Black Panther Party: "There's no more neutrality in the world. You either have to be part of the solution, or you're going to be part of the problem." I still didn't know the solution, but I saw the problem. Opposing it wasn't a solution in itself, but it was a beginning.

No sooner had we returned to Venice than the LA Panthers said they were ready to make themselves available for a documentary that would lay out their Marxist class analysis of the black struggle and emphasis their community programs. We were ready. Ron had a treatment keying off the assassinations of John and Bunchy called *Two Revolutionary Brothers*. We started researching and finding footage we could "borrow" from other documentaries and photo collections to show the history of oppression and the worldwide outbreak of revolutionary movements. Raw black-and-white film stock was cheap, and a film lab, sympathetic to our project, promised us a cut rate for developing and printing the film. While I continued to take our documentaries out and talk to groups, I agreed to film and edit this project with Mike's help. In spite of his occasional paranoid assertions and my own concerns about the nature of the Panther organization, he and I began filming with my trusty sixteen-millimeter Arriflex camera.

It was clear to all that our film wasn't going to emphasize Panthers with guns. *Off the Pig*, the earlier Newsreel film on the Oakland Panthers, was filled with militant images of grim-faced black men and a few women. From the beginning, the Panthers had demonstrated that bearing arms and defending their community was the right of every black American. Now, at least publicly, the message was slightly different. The Black Panther Party's influence extended far beyond Oakland. It was no longer limited to standing up to police brutality; it was a political organization, not unlike the Viet Cong, and like them, the Panthers were up against an imperialist power. While there had been no change to its militancy, and "Off the pig!" was chanted at every demonstration, they wanted to show they represented the whole range of needs and interests of the black community and welcomed working with all races.

That was the idea, but the Panthers in Los Angeles knew too well that the police and FBI were eager for any excuse to shoot at them. They told us about constant harassment, getting yanked out of their cars and rudely searched and arrested. They'd get released within days, but a good deal of the money they raised went into the bail fund. Since Bunchy and John had been killed in January, there had been several violent clashes, and we'd heard that some rank and file members had been killed. Ominously, back in April a few hundred heavily armed police had surrounded the LA headquarters and then withdrew once those inside alerted the local television stations of an impending bloodbath. The cops had forgotten to cut the phone lines, but few felt they would always be that stupid.

The Panthers had to organize and plan at two levels. They were "getting ready for the pigs" while, at the same time, they were expanding the breakfast program, planning a free health clinic in Bunchy's name, teaching self-defense classes, and bringing their views on political history into Watts and the surrounding communities.

Mike and I filmed kids chowing down on scrambled eggs and sausage at the Breakfast for Children program in Watts. Unfortunately, we weren't there to film the morning the police raided that same program and tried to intimidate the Panthers enough to shut it down. But the community desperately wanted it, and somehow the Panthers kept the program going. We covered the Panthers holding a rally in a neighborhood park as cop cars circled. We conducted a long, thoughtful interview with Masai Hewitt on the Panther philosophy.

The summer of 1969 was coming to an end, and unlike previous years, there hadn't been any major racial explosions nationwide. Although beyond their control, this fit with the Panthers' philosophy: Burning down your community was understandable emotionally, but self-defeating. It went without saying that the Panthers missed Bunchy. There were very few individuals who had been able to bring these angry warriors together under one banner like Bunchy Carter had in Los Angeles and Fred Hampton was doing at that time in Chicago, but tensions between the gangs had continued to subside. The Black Power movement had matured in size, confidence, and sophistication. Across the country, the Panthers were growing and expanding like mad. In Los Angeles, Newsreel was gathering the story.

※

Two strikingly contradictory sides of the Cultural Revolution went on display in August of 1969. A grotesque mix of revolutionary madness and "Do your own thing" resulted in an acid-fueled murder rampage that gripped Los Angeles in early August. It was the work of a psychopath named Charles Manson and his followers, who were trying to set off a racial apocalypse that, he insisted, the Beatles had forecast in their song "Helter Skelter." Flower Power was revealed to have a deadly, poisonous side.

Yet, within days, a wondrous demonstration of the loving, communal aspect of our times unfolded as nearly 500,000 people gathered for three days at an "Aquarian Exposition" on a farm in upstate New York. Woodstock! By all accounts it was an extraordinary experience of peace and harmony.

I didn't regret missing it. I'd had my mind blown at Monterey, and besides, my attention was on the political. The war was even more unpopular, and the entire basis for it, the 1964 Gulf of Tonkin "attack" on our destroyers by the North Vietnamese, was being seriously challenged. A letter was sent to the *New Haven Register* in Connecticut from John White, a former naval officer on the *U.S.S. Pine Island*. This was the first American ship to enter the war zone in response to the "attack" on the destroyers *Maddox* and *Turner Joy*. In speaking with the sonar man on the *Maddox*, White learned that the North Vietnamese had not fired any shells or torpedoes at U.S. warships. White claimed that the sonar man had "consistently reported this to the commanding officer during the 'attack.'" White concluded,

"I maintain that President Johnson, Secretary McNamara, and the Joint Chiefs of Staff gave false information to Congress in their report about U.S. destroyers being attacked in the Gulf of Tonkin."

This, as well as similar claims by those in the anti-war movement, were ignored and denied. It wasn't surprising that more and more people were convinced that the American government had fabricated the Gulf of Tonkin incident. LBJ, not North Vietnam, had started this madness, and we had another reason not to trust any politicians, whether Democrat or Republican.

I hadn't spoken with my father for over six months, so I gave him a call. Both our birthdays had passed without acknowledgment because we agreed that birthdays were arbitrary, commercial constructs that fostered a false sense of intimacy. We were our own sentimentality police.

Unlike Paul, my dad had never put much energy into arguing about politics. I doubted that he'd see things as cut-and-dried as I did, but I wanted his point of view. After I tried to explain myself, the recently retired businessman repeated an old adage that described his own political growth: "A man who's not a socialist when he's young has no heart, and a man who's a socialist when he's older has no brain."

"So, you're suggesting that I'm an idiot?" I said lightly.

"No. I'm only saying that one's perspective changes."

"Well, if 'young' means in my twenties, that leaves me only three years to overthrow the State," I responded.

He laughed, I'm sure at my presumption of such power, and said that I'd figure out how to come to terms with a conflict that he saw as commonplace in human history. "And keep in mind," he concluded with his recently acquired Buddhist perspective, "reality is only an illusion."

It sounded to me like the old Catholic had adopted an Eastern version of "Don't do anything stupid and we'll all meet in Heaven." I wanted to yell at him and lay bare the avoidant, self-serving nonsense he was spouting, but the gulf suddenly felt too great.

By Labor Day, I decided to get a broader perspective on how people perceived what was going on, and concocted a plan with Stef to take some films to show around the Southwest for ten days. We wouldn't call it a vacation; that was too bourgeois. But no one could complain if we helped open the SDS office at the University of Arizona in Tucson with a special screening. We grabbed some films, made sure we had everything necessary for camping, and set off across the desert. After the screening I spoke to nearly fifty kids crammed into their office, students eager to radicalize their corner of the world. Stef wasn't comfortable speaking to large groups, but she was extremely effective one-on-one. Afterward, we were invited to a commune out in the desert and got stoned with dozens more who were determined to evolve a new society. We made sweet love while a thunderstorm dropped a cobweb of lightning on the surrounding mountains, and fell asleep as the monsoon rains drummed wildly on the roof of the van.

An acquaintance told us to look up a labor organizer in Albuquerque. He invited us to show the films at a retreat of campus workers from the University of New Mexico who were preparing for a strike. In what had become a common Newsreel practice, I stopped in the middle of some films and asked how it related to their situation. As usual the audience was brought into the moment even more. After a spirited and moving two days discussing issues with the Chicano workers, we moved on to Denver and the Crusade for Justice run by Corky Gonzales. We screened *Salt of the Earth*, a progressive dramatic film made in the 1950s that the government had tried to sabotage. The Chicano audience was inspired by the story of the Mexican and white miners overcoming the violent attempts by the mining corporation to break the strikers' spirit.

Speaking afterward, I underscored the point that that the success of the strike was due to the wives of the miners overcoming management's efforts to divide the workers along racial lines. "Women belong in a leadership role," I said, "then and now."

I was followed by Corky Gonzalez, the head of the organization, who thanked us for showing the film, but went on to insist that women better served social change from the vantage point of the kitchen and with the children. I could feel the tension in the room. In the social hour afterward, Stef and I realized from many different conversations that the movie had made its points well. Our time there demonstrated that, if handled respectfully, there was a broad intersection where politics jibed even though cultures clashed. As we had observed many times by then, such was the power of film and discussion.

We were turned on in all sorts of ways. Besides having a romantic road trip, in less than two weeks, we'd personally shown films and spoken with over five hundred people. We helped to organize and raise consciousness among students in Arizona, workers in New Mexico, and the Chicano community in Denver. I felt on fire and once back in LA I continued to show films like crazy.

The trial of the Chicago 7 began on September 24th. It had been the Chicago 8, but Bobby Seale, national chairman of the Panthers, severed his trial from the others. To many, it was as if the whole antiwar movement and the legitimacy of protest were on trial. The courtroom immediately became the setting for myriad political and racial issues to be debated. On several occasions, the trial turned into a circus with Abbie Hoffman as ringmaster, which set up the legal system for ridicule. It went on for weeks.

To show solidarity with the defendants, the Weatherman contingent of SDS decided to "bring the war home." They had been organizing among the alienated, proletarian white kids in the high schools and streets of Chicago. They were convinced that these kids, and thousands of others across America, only needed a spark to rise up and revolt against the system. They ardently believed that provocative actions connected to the outrageousness of the trial could be that spark. Young white Americans, like them, had had enough. Talk hadn't changed shit. It was time for "exemplary action." They sent out the call: Come to Chicago, October 8–11, 1969, for the Days of Rage.

None of LA Newsreel went. Everyone experienced the impulse to take action against the government, felt the emotional appeal, understood the need. But to pick a fight in the streets with well-armed cops and, probably, National Guard, with the idea that thousands of pissed-off, disenfranchised white kids would be inspired to join in? That seemed nuts, a revolutionary fantasy. We already had enough American kids getting killed in Vietnam in a losing cause. Why duplicate that in Chicago?

Instead of the few thousand they expected, 350 angry rebels were on hand the first night. They finally gathered their courage and started taking out their "rage" through the streets of Chicago, breaking windows in homes, businesses, and police cars. Two thousand cops were ready. They shot at them—hitting six—bashed them with nightsticks, and drove squad cars into their midst. It didn't inspire others to join them in the streets, but for the first time, it made it clear to a significant number of these white, burgeoning revolutionaries that it was time to go underground. It didn't set off a revolution, but it created the makings of a guerilla war.

With schools back in session, it was anti-war demonstration season. First up was a new approach to indicating how unpopular the war was: a daylong "Strike for Peace." Ever since I had marched in the first anti-war demonstration in Manhattan in 1965, protests had been held in big cities like New York, San Francisco, and Washington, D.C., to amass the most people and create the strongest sense of a movement. But this time the plan was for a one-day Vietnam Moratorium in towns and cities across the country. The message was simple: Stop business as usual in order to show disapproval of the war, and demand Nixon bring the troops home. The Vietnam Moratorium Committee coordinated 253 student newspaper editors and student-government officers nationwide who pledged to get the word out. Students went door to door in their college-town neighborhoods. Adults were ready to talk to these clean-cut, earnest kids, part of the generation they'd read were unpatriotic and morally corrupt. It was hard to slam the door when the students opened the conversation through the screen door with something like, "There are currently over 500,000 American boys fighting in Vietnam. President Nixon has said he'll withdraw 25,000 for now. At this rate, we will still be in Vietnam in nine years." People talked, listened, debated, and on the 15th of October, two million of them across the country joined the "Strike for Peace," most protesting for the first time in their lives.

That night, the phone woke me up. Over the clinking of money dropping into a pay phone, Baseball Billy's drunken voice exulted, "World Series alert! The audacious, no-talent, miraculous New York Mets are up three to one over the all-mighty Orioles. And here's the bitchin'-est part: Tom Seaver, tonight's winning pitcher, said, 'If the Mets can get to the World Series, the U.S. can get out of Vietnam.'"

A hollow crashing sound indicated he'd dropped the phone and the line went dead. The next day, Toby, one of my new friends from D.C. Newsreel, called to read me the headline from the *Washington Post*: "Anti-Vietnam Views Unite Generations." He was flipped out by how mainstream the anti-war movement had become. *Life* magazine wrote that the Moratorium was "the largest expression of public dissent ever seen in this country." All President Nixon could muster was that he hadn't seen a single demonstrator and that he wouldn't be swayed by demonstrations. The public was not impressed, and support for Nixon and the war dropped.

In the following days, Nixon struck back wildly through his vice president, Spiro Agnew. Agnew attacked anti-war intellectuals as "an effete corps of impudent snobs." Anti-war leaders were "political hustlers" and "vultures" who "prey upon the good intentions of gullible men everywhere." He lambasted liberals who supported insurrectionists like Eldridge Cleaver, who had predicted that the "complacent regime" of imperial America would fall within our lifetime. Agnew asked, "Will citizens refuse to be led by a series of Judas goats down tortuous paths to delusion and self-destruction?" Clearly a lot of citizens were being led to radical conclusions about America, or he wouldn't have asked the question.

After having Agnew, his evil doppelganger, blame the anti-war movement for the nation's problems, the President then attempted to cast himself as the one who would avoid the shame of "the first defeat in our nation's history." Another massive demonstration was quickly approaching on November 15, 1969. Ten days before the New Mobilization Against the War ("New Mobe") gathered in Washington, D.C., Nixon declared he'd found a new way out: "Vietnamization." Already, he claimed, the retraining of South Vietnamese troops would allow him to bring 20% of American soldiers home before the year's end. But in order to be "united for peace" as well as "united against defeat," he asked for the support of "the great—silent—majority of my fellow Americans."

Most of the news commentators said they didn't see that this approach was much different from previous failed efforts to end the war. Nixon was furious and decided to go after the media itself. He asked the three networks to air a speech of Agnew's just two days before the New Mobe's "March Against Death." Agnew used this speech to attack the three big TV networks. He complained that the seventy million Americans who had tuned into the President's "Vietnamization" speech the week before had "the right to make up their own minds and form their own opinions about a presidential address without having the President's words and thoughts characterized through the prejudices of hostile critics before they can even be digested." Agnew concluded with a chilling logic: "The American people would rightly not tolerate this kind of concentration of power in government. Is it not fair and relevant to question its concentration in the hands of a tiny and closed fraternity of privileged men, elected by no one, and enjoying a monopoly sanctioned and licensed by government?" While everyone had complaints about the media, it had a whole different effect when the government itself complained that a powerful cabal controlled it.

The networks were outraged. Walter Cronkite called it an "implied threat to freedom of speech," and his boss at CBS sharpened the point by saying it was an attempt to intimidate those whose existence depends upon a government license. But they got the message. They caved in. Two days later, there was no live TV coverage of what was estimated to be nearly 400,000 people who gathered in Washington at the New Mobe demonstration, nor of the 9,000 troops guarding the besieged center of our government, including Marines manning a machine-gun nest right on the Capitol steps.

"If this isn't the act of a fascist state, I don't know what is," said Toby, who called again from the D.C. Newsreel office to tell us how many angry citizens showed up to protest and do civil disobedience. But a lot fewer people saw it, and Nixon had put lightning in a bottle with his phrase "the silent majority," and by portraying himself as striving for peace. I couldn't believe it, but the public polls turned around and the body politic seemed to find new patience and trust in a man who, it was painfully clear to the rest of us, deserved neither. To us, there was scarcely a shadow of our system worth saving.

However uncertain I was about how radical I was going to be, others had decided and were taking action. Four day before the New Mobe march in D.C., bombs went off in the deserted offices of Chase Manhattan Bank, Standard Oil, and General Motors, and a day later at the Manhattan Criminal Courts Building. Violence-prone munchkins were trying to pull the curtain and reveal the wizards of industry who were really running things.

"Fuck me, fuck me," Bill muttered from behind the *New York Times* he was reading. He dropped the paper onto his lap. "The FBI arrested four people for those bombings last week, including Herman Grossman, my old friend. He once tried to drop barrels from the roof on top of the pigs during the Columbia takeover. Almost got us killed."

"Did you know he'd moved on to real bombs?" Barbara asked.

"No," Bill said quickly, "but I'd hate to have to convince the feds of that."

"Do they have any way to connect you to him?" I asked.

"Columbia, lots of meetings, rallies, parties…he was far out, so was I. We agreed that certain provocations would appeal to the most conscious members of the working class, and that would build support for revolution. But shit, it seems that most of the working class say they still support that pig Nixon."

"I'm not so sure," Tim said. "Between the bombings and the millions of people protesting the war in the last month, I bet that Nixon is really losing it."

Tim had reason to worry. During that summer of 1969 through early fall, Nixon had been warning North Vietnam that he'd bomb them to dust by November 1 if they didn't soften their negotiation demands at the Paris talks. But they didn't. It must have been clear to the President that massive bombing would have brought out even more immense demonstrations at home. At the same time, he no doubt feared he was looking vulnerable to the Russians and North Vietnamese, and he was convinced they'd never negotiate with him if he seemed weak. How far would he go to convince them he was crazy enough to really start bombing them? We could only wonder.

The next time Bill and I went to screen films at the Panther office, the effect of the violent tactics of the Weathermen became personal. We'd just shown *San Francisco State*, a new documentary by San Francisco Newsreel about the five-month student strike that had resulted in a Black Studies Program and other progressive changes amid police brutality and racial tension. Geronimo Pratt, the LA Minister of Defense, got up in front and directed a pointed question to Bill and me in the back with the projector. "I want to know what our white comrades here thought about the role of the white students supporting the brothers' efforts to get rid of the racist policies of that so-called institution of higher learning?"

"Well, of course we support that…"

"There's no 'of course' around these issues," Geronimo interrupted. Even when he wasn't upset, as he was now, Geronimo was intimidating. Like several other Panthers, he was an ex-Marine who had served multiple tours in Vietnam and didn't suffer fools. "Not since some of your damn white brothers decided to go out and raise hell on their own, which brought down all sorts of sorrow on the black residents of Chicago."

"You're talking about the Days of Rage last month?" I began.

"Goddamn right! I'm talking about some white wannabe revolutionaries. Weathermen," he sneered the word through the air, "who forgot they were tripping out in a black neighborhood, which gave the Chicago pig force an excuse to break down doors and haul poor black people out into the night and beat the shit out of them. Now, what I want to know is, what do you think of that?"

"It's ridiculous," I began as Bill said, "They're stupid motherfuckers."

Geronimo shook his head, dissatisfied with our shallow analysis. "In a moment I'll read you what Fred Hampton, our Black Panther chairman in Chicago, said." He addressed the rapt audience: "You should all be aware that brother Hampton had been friendly with our Weatherman allies until this point. He, our founder Huey Newton, and our dearly missed brother Bunchy were of one brilliant mind. Brother Fred is another example of why the pigs will never defeat the Black Panther Party. There will always be another leader to take the reins of the organization. It might be one of you some day."

A steely, determined stillness fell over the closely packed room. "What we have learned from these brothers is that we are political revolutionaries, not gangsters or Black Nationalists, and there are roles for people of all races in our march to bring down the pig power structure. Fred and Bunchy each brought thousands of their gang brothers into the light of understanding. Brother Fred created what he called a 'rainbow coalition' of black and brown gangs along with white SDS members. But," and here he looked at us directly as he brought out the Panther newspaper, "in regards to this particular event, he wrote, 'We believe that the Weather action was anarchistic, opportunistic, individualistic, chauvinistic, and…'" He stopped and smiled. "This is why I love this brother. He called it 'Custeristic,' and then the brother added, 'It's nothing but child's play—it's folly.'"

Many of the assembled recruits laughed and called out, "Right on!" Geronimo put the paper down and continued with, "This self-inflated, Custeristic bullshit on the part of certain white radicals has not only caused problems for the black community, but it's made trouble in our own party." He glared at Bill and me. "That's why we need to be sure that our own white comrades understand who's leading this revolutionary cause."

"I don't know what other trouble you're talking about, but we know who the vanguard is," I said. "That's why we're here supporting you."

"Right on!" he nodded, apparently satisfied. "If you had read the Panther newspaper, as these brothers and sisters do every week, you'd know that the 'problem' is that brother Eldridge Cleaver, who's been forced by this jive-assed legal system to relocate and join the international movement in Algeria, called out Brother Hampton for criticizing our white comrades. His point was that any attack on the pig power structure was right on, and you never criticize the enemy of your enemy. He said Brother Hampton needed to apologize and respect the Panthers' coalition with white radical groups. Well, the brother did meet with the offended Weatherman contingent led by Bernardine Dohrn. No doubt encouraged by Brother Cleaver's statements, they were looking for an apology. Not only did Brother Hampton refuse but he kicked them out after a very nasty argument."

Shouts of agreement erupted, but Geronimo silenced the crowd. "The Black Panther Central Committee agrees with Brother Hampton. And here's the big news, that brother has been asked to join the Central Committee as chief of staff and act as national spokesman for the Black Panther Party."

At this, the audience stood with rousing cheers of "Right on!" and the meeting was over.

Bill and I stayed after to be sure the leadership in LA was truly comfortable working with us. Masai assured us things were cool. He mentioned that Fred Hampton had recently spoken at the UCLA Law Students Association and that while he was away from Chicago, some Panthers got into a shoot-out with the police. Two officers were killed and nine more shot. One Panther was killed. "It's not just Chicago," he said in his soft voice. "I think you met Toure during the summer?" We nodded. "You may not have heard that he and Bruce were pulled over on October tenth and a gunfight broke out. Toure's dead."

"Goddamn, that's fucked up!" Bill said.

"I'm really sorry, man," I said.

Masai nodded. "The pigs are pissed off, and an angry pig will charge you at any time."

In a side room we saw several men cleaning rifles. One young man whom I'd gotten to know a bit smiled with pride when he looked up. Then he quickly grew serious and returned to his duty.

"Anything you can get to help us fortify would be appreciated," Masai said as we stepped past some sandbags stacked near the front door on our way out.

Masai's informal request and the recent deaths finally forced me to confront the degree of militancy I was ready to assume. I no longer had faith in nonviolence. I wasn't sure I ever had, especially since I'd grown up hunting. But hunting was a far cry from military action. I was ready to do more, but what? Stanley's searching question rang in my head. I was certainly a lot closer to hating enough to consider Weatherman-type actions. But without the existence of some sort of "United Front," random guerilla action only stirred up more problems for the people. Still, I had to act, had to do something other than analyze the contradictions.

The next night Peter and I "liberated" a dozen thick sheets of plywood from a construction site in the Marina and took them across town in my van. Peter surprised me when he revealed that he and Jonathan had recently taken the Panthers other "supplies." Evidently, this kind of support was up to each individual and didn't call for a collective decision. We pulled up on Central Avenue at midnight and tapped at the frosted windows. Peaches, one of the few women I'd come to know, cautiously opened the door. Immediately, Cotton and two more men whose names I didn't know came out and helped us bring the wood into the front office. The entire front of the building was now covered with sandbags from floor to ceiling. The wood was evidently going to be used for reinforcing other walls and ceilings. The drop-off was done in near silence, the atmosphere tense but not grim. There was work to do—preparations for battle, should it come. With a few exchanges of the clenched fist salute, we were headed back to the relative safety of west Los Angeles in less than five minutes. Those iconic phrases, at once a demand and a wish, hung in the chilly, early winter air: "Power to the people. Right on."

15

REPRESSION

In December of 1969, the government lived up to its fascist reputation via two spectacular, audacious attacks. In Chicago on December 4, heavily armed police raided an apartment where Fred Hampton was sleeping and riddled him and another Panther, Matt Clark, with bullets. After an initial half-baked "investigation," the cops swaggered away from the scene and failed to secure the site. For several days, the stunned Chicago Panthers invited the community to see the atrocity for themselves. The walls bore testimony to the fact that all but one bullet hole came from where the police entered and stood. This and other evidence indicated a premeditated murder by the state. They hadn't even set up intermediaries like the US organization to do their dirty work.

We were still reeling from the news when, in the predawn darkness of December 8, only the barking dogs in the neighborhood alerted the eleven Panthers sleeping in their LA office that something malevolent was coming their way. The SWAT team, a newly created paramilitary "anti-insurrectionist" force of the LA Police Department, announced their desire to serve a warrant by knocking down their front door with a battering ram.

This initial assault on the Panthers' headquarters at 41st and Central Ave met strong resistance, and the SWAT team requested the additional firepower of hundreds of police. Soon the community and news media gathered to watch. Tear gas was poured in and the roof was bombed from a helicopter. This army of cops traded gunfire for five hours with the Panthers inside, seven of them teenagers. Sandbags in the walls, below the roof, and under the ceilings protected them from most of the five thousand rounds of ammunition poured into the building. Miraculously, no one was killed. Maybe it shouldn't have been surprising: Well-trained, ex-U.S. Marines had designed the Panther defense.

At 10:00 a.m., once their ammunition ran out, Peaches courageously emerged, waving a white flag. She and the ten others survived, but all of them faced charges of conspiracy to murder police officers and possession of illegal weapons. That attack was just one of three simultaneous, early-morning raids at sites the LA Panthers were known to live or gather.

Cops and well over a hundred people from the community were still nervously milling around the ruined headquarters when Mike and I arrived an hour later. I climbed the stairs at the back of the building with my Arriflex purring and filmed the splintered hole that had been blasted in the roof. I peered in. A large mound of dirt blocked the back door. For weeks they'd been digging a tunnel to access the sewer system as a way to escape, but it hadn't been finished. Still, the dirt pile stopped the cops from storming through the back and attacking them from the front and back. Planning and luck in equal parts saved lives on both sides. But my side lost, and its future—the Panther Party's future—suddenly felt very much in question.

The smell of the tear gas lingered. My eyes stung; my stomach was in knots. It wasn't clear what I was shooting film for. Only a few weeks earlier, Mike and I had shown a rough cut to the accolades of our Newsreel comrades. Obviously, it could be updated, but I had a sinking feeling that our film had been turned into an historical artifact, irrelevant to the present.

I looked out over South-Central LA from the roof. I fantasized gangs sprouting up in the streets and spreading out in full force. They would be divided once again by race and geography, and they'd kill one another fighting over crumbs. The future for a young black or brown man and his community would shrink for want of the Panthers' inspired vision of brotherhood.

I heard movement and turned as a cop came onto the roof. "What're you doing up here?" he demanded.

"Obviously I'm filming what happened."

He clearly didn't like the look of my tattered leather jacket, long hair, and beard. "Let's see some ID."

For fun, Mike and I had cooked up plastic-covered Newsreel IDs. My picture was backlit and my hair flared out like I was flying. I looked like a madman, but it did have **PRESS** stamped on it and the office address. I certainly wasn't from CBS, but it was just official-looking enough. The cop passed it back to me with disdain and told me I better watch my step. "This neighborhood's not safe for a white guy. These blacks are armed and don't care who they kill," he said. Apparently, I was an ally as long as I accepted his racist version of our society. He stared at me a moment as though his guys hadn't started this battle. I had no hope of influencing him and simply shrugged as he stomped back down the stairs.

The crisis over civil rights, Vietnam, and social unrest that had already driven a sitting President from office had fueled a hidden reaction in the government that was at odds with the core values and laws that America supposedly stood for. If it hadn't been clear before, it was now obvious that the government was in attack mode on its home ground. Any radical black leader who was truly charismatic and was having success organizing was killed. John and Bunchy and Fred Hampton were three obvious examples. Many among us would point to Martin Luther King, Jr. as well, especially once his civil rights message included an anti-war element. Whether MLK deserved to be on that list or not, it was clear the FBI and other governmental agencies were intent on destroying the most radical elements of our society by any means, legal or not. The rest of us they would continue to infiltrate and disrupt, as many SDS chapters, anti-war organizations, New York Newsreel, and innumerable veteran, pacifist, and religious organizations could attest. Many believed that double agents were the ones urging them on to more and more radical and violent forms of protest. Once in a while, a police or FBI agent was discovered. But too often they were successful.

Around the time of the raid on the LA Panther headquarters, Tim had told me, "Two guys in suits came by the office asking for you. They didn't show badges, but they said they were FBI." It hadn't surprised me. While we were too small a group to infiltrate with ease, we assumed they were looking for ways to mess with us.

The holidays sent students home, and screenings dropped off for a couple of weeks. It was a somber time: The "Merry" had been blasted out of "Merry Christmas." When the LA Newsreel collective gathered in January of 1970, Mike and I showed everyone the footage of the aftermath of the raid on the Panthers.

As it ended, Mike flipped on the lights. It was obvious that new circumstances had put the entire project in jeopardy. "I feel like we're caught in a weird sort of madness now," I ventured. "The elders in our society have begun to devour their young."

Jonathan was not one for poetic sentimentality. "Age has nothing to do with it. It's about ideology. The murders of Fred Hampton and Matt Clark were the latest in a string of political assassinations. They were the twenty-seventh and twenty-eighth Panthers to be killed in the last two years! The destruction of the Panther headquarters here in LA was another politically motivated attack by a fascist state. And, as much as we all hate to admit it, those fuckers have been successful."

An awkward silence fell over the meeting until he added, "We've been trying to help the Panthers in all sorts of ways, but if we are realistic, we have to accept that the future of the revolution can't be made dependent on their fate."

"Wrong, Jonathan!" Ron interrupted. " The Panthers are flooded with new recruits. They're not only relevant, they're growing."

"Liberals are freaked out, "Barbara added. "Money is pouring in from them along with hundreds of thousands of dollars more in small donations from the black communities."

Bill shook the latest copy of the Black Panther newspaper. "Eldridge Cleaver says now is the time for mad men! He's ready to go to war."

So was Custer, I thought. Bill added, "The Weather Underground claims to have bombed several police cars in Chicago two days after Hampton was killed."

"Hey, Bill," I broke in. "Don't forget that Fred Hampton criticized the Weathermen and Cleaver's support of them just a few months ago. Neither he nor the LA Panthers wanted anything to do with their Custeristic bullshit."

Judy took the floor, bouncing baby Lola on her hip. "There's a lot of brave talk, but the Weathermen are going to get innocent people killed, and Eldridge Cleaver is hiding out in Algeria. It won't be obvious for a while, maybe a year, but the vanguard has been vanquished." Lola began to protest. Peter got up and took her.

Once again several people disagreed, and we debated without resolution for a while. Then Judy declared, "History shows that revolution moves in stages. The Black Panthers represent the preliminary phase of our revolution. If their organization is weakened, or even destroyed, it means we've lost a battle, not the war. You wouldn't have to convince Huey Newton that it's going to take time to win against imperialism in Vietnam and fascism here at home."

As he walked back and forth with Lola, Peter agreed, "Our role must be more than recruiting for the Panthers. As for our film, we can revise the narrative and make it about repression in general."

Barbara said, "It feels like we're giving up on them."

"This is fucked up," Ron declared.

"No way are we giving up," Jonathan said. "This repression creates all the more reason to make a deeper commitment to the class nature of the struggle. Let's not forget the conversation we've been having about moving the office out of this bourgeois west side of LA.

We've all agreed that it's messed up, almost counter-revolutionary, that people from the working-class neighborhoods in central and east LA have a hard time getting our films."

Elinor spoke up, "Christine, Jonathan and I found a house in Watts where some of us can live with plenty of room for an office. It'll take a month or two to work out, but I say we do it." She looked around the room. "Anyone disagree?"

"It's okay with me," I said. "But since the rest of us will still be living around Venice, it could make coordinating screenings and speakers a real pain in the ass."

"I've been working in this office more than anyone and I know we can work that out," Tim responded. "But relocating the office is just a cosmetic change. The real problem is, if the Panthers are no longer the vanguard, what the hell are we supposed to say when we show films?"

A strained silence took hold until Jonathan stood and said, "That's the question and we're not the first ones in history to confront it." He pulled out a thin pamphlet with a picture of Lenin on the cover. "We need to start studying *What Is To Be Done?* and others Marxist works. Marv Treiger said he'd lead the discussion if we commit to weekly meetings."

Marv was a librarian, a thin, devoted Marxist with a wispy Ho Chi Minh beard who'd been a strong supporter of LA Newsreel from the beginning. Whenever he showed up, he'd deliver a brief and illuminating Marxist analysis of the nature of the state under capitalism.

"I see," Mike spoke up, "it's the librarians who will take state power and run the show." We all laughed and he added with cutting sarcasm, "How about we just make a pilgrimage to Lenin's tomb once a year?"

"If you want anarchy, you should join the Weathermen," Jonathan interrupted the laughter.

"Fuck off, Jonathan," Mike shot back. "That's like some simpleton from the John Birch Society telling you to go back to Russia if you don't like it here."

Jonathan barely managed a shrug of apology, then continued. "The FBI isn't going to let up on people advocating armed revolution. The Panthers are associated with guns, but they're in no position to begin real guerilla warfare. This isn't Vietnam, and the Panthers don't have the kind of support that the Viet Cong have."

"You mean because they're black they can't disappear into white communities for protection," Barbara said, "'like fish into the sea,' as Chairman Mao says. And there's no white guerilla movement, so…"

"So it's either the Weathermen or the librarians," Mike finished.

Ron interrupted, "This country is nowhere near ready for a class revolution and it's insane to consider it."

⁂

Eventually, this argument over the future of the political movement would cause Barbara and Ron to leave the collective, clear evidence that Newsreel wasn't immune to the factionalizing that plagued the left in general. And, after this debate, Mike stopped coming to meetings, though he and I stayed close as friends, neighbors, and fellow artists.

The rest felt that a study group that helped us develop a deeper theoretical understanding of the conditions that lead to revolution could be helpful. We went back out, armed with our films, and along with the rest of the anti-war movement, hammered on the hypocrisy of Nixon declaring that he was working for peace. But the situation was beginning to change: Nixon's "Vietnamization" and his pose as a peacemaker improved his position in the polls. Even more disturbing, we had the feeling that his recent replacement of the draft with a lottery system was diminishing the fervor of the student movement. This underscored a frustrating reality: To the extent that the anti-war and student movements drove the revolutionary effort in the U.S., it was vulnerable to falling apart as the threat of being drafted diminished. This was true even though the war still raged. Over 100,000 soldiers had been brought home, but 400,000 continued to fight in our name, killing not only soldiers, but as the Mỹ Lai massacre made clear, innocent women and children.

For many, the situation had become intolerable, and it was ripping America apart. Tim was usually our most anxious Newsreel comrade, occasionally sounding an alarm like the canary in the mine. He served that function on Wednesday, February 18, 1970, the day the verdicts for the trial of the Chicago 7 were announced. Several of us sat over beers at Brandelli's Brig down the street from our office. Barely audible over the sound of laughter and ball-busting at the pool table, he pointed out, "I hope you guys appreciate how serious this is. Five of the Chicago 7 were found guilty of traveling over state lines and speaking to groups of people for the purpose of inciting, organizing, promoting, and encouraging a riot."

"At least they weren't found guilty of conspiracy," Elinor said.

"That's not the point. How are you going to feel the next time you go out with some films and people get excited and burn a trash can or break some windows? It's happening all over, and as speakers, we could be arrested."

We knew he was right. Students and radicals of all ages had lost patience. It wasn't just the Weathermen doing shit; aggressive, violent reactions against police and property had become common in anti-war demonstrations. Whether driven by moral outrage, belief in anarchy or Marxism, there were a lot of people across the country determined to stop business as usual. The power of Gandhi and Martin Luther King Jr.'s nonviolent approach was no longer "blowin' in the wind." Five thousand students and "rabble-rousers," as the administration liked to call them, marched to city hall in Ann Arbor, Michigan, breaking windows and destroying cars. From February 12–21, a student strike forced the governor of Wisconsin to call out the National Guard just to keep the University of Wisconsin campus at Madison open.

On February 20, the night of the homecoming football game at the University of California at Santa Barbara, I showed films and spoke to over four hundred kids at the UCSB auditorium. On February 23,

William Kunstler, attorney for the Chicago 7, who was already facing two years in jail for contempt of Judge Hoffman's court, spoke on the same campus and said that although he didn't think "sporadic, picayune violence is a good tactic," he couldn't "condemn young people who engage in it." On February 25, the students rioted and burned down the Bank of America branch on campus. Governor Reagan was incensed. He told his Attorney General to see if he could charge Kunstler with crossing state lines to incite a riot. I was sure there were FBI agents at my speech at homecoming and couldn't help but wonder if I'd be charged.

On March 6, an explosion destroyed a townhouse in Manhattan's Greenwich Village. Three members of a Weatherman collective blew themselves up as they tried to construct a bomb made from dynamite wrapped with nails as shrapnel. They had evidently intended to set it off at a non-com officers' dance in nearby Fort Dix, New Jersey. Their demise must have shocked others of similar mind, but it didn't seem to demoralize them. In fact, it inspired them. In New York City later that same month, over three hundred bomb threats were made, causing fifteen thousand people to be evacuated from office buildings.

On April 4, in a speech while campaigning for reelection, California Governor Ronald Reagan said about stemming the increasing violence, "If there is to be a bloodbath, let it be now."

Jerry Rubin, one of the Chicago 7, was touring the nation to tout his new book, *Do It*. He'd given a copy to the trial's judge, inscribed, "Julius Hoffman, top Yippie, who radicalized more young Americans than we ever could." On April 10, Rubin threw down a hauntingly radical gauntlet to over fifteen hundred students. He said, "The first part of the Yippie program is to kill your parents. And I mean that quite literally, because until you're prepared to kill your parents, you're not prepared to change this country." He was speaking at Kent State in Ohio.

Over chicken adobo at the Zamboanga Cafe, Mike told me what Rubin had said. He couldn't help but gloat. "It's starting to happen, man. A state of permanent revolution is taking hold."

I was rattled by his glib assessment and asked, "Did you ever hear that Buddhist saying, 'If you see the Buddha on the road, kill him'?" He shook his head. "It's a koan, like the little movie we made. To me, it means that if you think you find the answer while on your path through life, kill it, forget it. Perfection is an illusion. But Jerry Rubin has hijacked Buddhism into the realm of politics and it's insane. He not only has no sense of the metaphor he's using, he's playing with other people's lives. I mean, look what happened in the Cultural Revolution in China."

Mike sat back and considered my opinion. Finally, he asked, "And you're not playing with people's lives?"

"Not like that, and I'm sure not playing at being an American Chairman Mao telling kids to bring me their parents' heads."

"No, but you're acting like you've got the answer to our problems: take down Nixon; replace capitalism with socialism led by smart, kind workers, and your headache will disappear. However, according to your Zen masters, there really is no answer." Mike chortled at the philosophical conundrum he'd put me into. "We'll just have to wait and see which comes first: you reach enlightenment, the country stops being an imperialist bully, or socialism brings communal bliss."

"The point is that you can't grasp enlightenment, if there is such a state."

"Well, that's a relief," he said and, for a change, picked up the bill.

It seemed that no one was interested in such philosophical subtleties, especially the President. Throughout his career he'd been labeled a two-faced liar, but the Vietnam War drove him to new depths. Although Nixon said he didn't want to become the first president to lose a war and would therefore negotiate his way out of it, it always seemed clear that what he really wanted was to win the damn thing. But he wasn't. Threatening North Vietnam with bombing them back to the Stone Age, and his "mad man" tactic in November of '69 to force North Vietnam to give in at the peace talks, had failed miserably. So, only five months later, he went on the military offensive while trying to make it look like he was winding the war down. On April 20, 1970, he proudly announced that the war effort had been so successful that he was withdrawing an additional 150,000 troops from Vietnam. The feeling that the anti-war movement was weakened was reinforced even more that same day as the Vietnam Moratorium announced it was shutting down operations. It said that demonstrations seemingly had too little effect on the administration. However, ten days later, on April 30, Nixon announced the bombing of Cambodia. Somehow he expected us to believe that Vietnamization was so successful that it required bombing and putting our ground troops in another country.

Demonstrations broke out all over, but the nation came completely unglued on May 4, when National Guardsmen opened fire on protestors, wounding nine and killing four white students at Kent State. College campuses went berserk. A worker at Case Western Reserve University where a ROTC building was burned down described the students' attitude to the *Wall Street Journal*: "They figure they might as well die here for something they believe in as to die in Vietnam." True enough, but a lot of Americans saw it differently. A few days after the killings, a Gallop poll found that 58% of respondents blamed the Kent State students for their own deaths, while a mere 11% blamed the National Guard.

I was reading the Los Angeles Times on the steps of my little cottage trying to digest this last piece of news when Mike stepped into the yard from his place. "Six out of ten people blame the kids who got shot!" I yelled as I shook the paper.

Mike approached, strangely subdued. "I just got off the phone with an old friend." He paused, "I was raised just down the road from Kent, in Akron." I nodded. "He told me a story that's going around about this mom who has three sons at Kent State. I thought I knew how rabid those folks could get, but," he paused again and stared off in space.

I rattled the paper to get him to continue. He ignored the golden-eyed dog that barked and glared menacingly at us. "She said that if anyone was on the streets of Kent with long hair and dirty clothes, or even barefooted, that they deserved to be shot. She fucking said that if her own kids didn't do what the Guard told them, they should have been mowed down. Man, she pushes patriotism to a Biblical level, like a menopausal Abraham." He tried to laugh, but it sounded like he'd been punched in the belly. "She told the reporter or whoever it was that we gotta clean up the nation and it should begin with the longhairs." He dropped down next to me on the step. We sat silently in the sun until he added, "What Jerry Rubin said about parents a few weeks ago in Kent? That crazy Yippie didn't know how right he was."

As usual, Newsreel members were out in the middle of the demonstrations, filming the action from the protestors' point of view rather than from behind the cops and Guardsmen. I was at UCLA as hundreds marched through the campus vandalizing buildings. The LAPD were called, bashed some heads, and arrested about seventy people. I had to assume my camera protected me, because the cops ignored me as they rushed past to chase down the students. Soon after, for the first time in history, Governor Reagan closed down California state colleges and universities.

In Manhattan on May 8, four days after Kent State, Mayor John Lindsey ordered flags at city hall to be at half-staff in honor of the dead students. There was an anti-war march, but this time about two hundred construction workers attacked and beat demonstrators while the police watched. It was quickly dubbed a "Hardhat Riot." That same day, National Guard at New Mexico State bayoneted eleven student protesters.

On the 10th of May, 100,000 people demonstrated against the Cambodian bombings in Washington, D.C., and it was violent. Nixon was squirreled away to Camp David for two days, while the Army's 82nd Airborne was assembled in the basement of the executive building ready for action. On May 14, two black students were killed and twelve injured at a protest at Jackson State in Jackson, Mississippi.

The reaction to Nixon's audacious expansion of the war spread over the entire country. If it wasn't civil war, as some suggested, it was at the very least a nation at war with itself.

Nixon's opinion was that those in the anti-war movement were the pawns of foreign communists. Those communists must have been mighty persuasive, because over four million students protested, and nearly half of them participated in the first nationwide student strike in history. Over 536 American colleges and universities shut down during the student strikes, many for the rest of the academic year. Like FJ suggested, the fantasy of a student-led revolution remained an alluring possibility. After all, how long could the military generals count on their young soldiers, whether National Guard or regular Army, to fire at other American kids who were pleading with them to join their ranks? And the anti-war sentiment wasn't just within the United States. Reports of "fragging" indicated it was getting harder to maintain discipline in Vietnam. It was impossible to know how widespread it was, but the possibility that soldiers were assassinating reckless or cowardly officers by tossing a fragmentation grenade at them during firefights had to shake up the military.

The more Nixon played the anti-communist card, the more I became a commie. I was certainly a fledgling Marxist, studying with a passion I rarely had in college and absorbing the arguments showing that capitalism was the basis for the rot in our system. There was a compelling logic behind the necessity to overthrow the system, and Nixon's paranoia only reinforced that conclusion. The sense was getting stronger that our president was willing to loose the dogs on white radicals with the same intensity as he had on those in the Black Power movement. Rumors abounded about informers, provocateurs, illegal electronic surveillance, and opening the mail of domestic "radicals." Many were convinced that camps were being created in Western states where anti-war protesters and others would be detained.

"Bring the War Home," the protest signs implored. It was.

16

LOVE

"Smoggy" was a random fifth season in Los Angeles. It was a wild card that could show up at any time to make breathing a pain. I'd often felt its gagging, smothering invasion in my chest as a painter in downtown LA. Moving to Venice Beach had brought a welcome relief. A thin, dung-yellow blanket might hover over LA all the way to the desert, yet the air would be fine at the seashore. But occasionally, a warm, dry Santa Ana wind from the east would push that acrid-smelling crap out over the water, where it would hang until an onshore breeze pushed it back to the freeways and factories where it was born.

For three days it had hung over us, but I'd sensed the weather change during the night. A tropical storm was moving up from Baja California, pushing the smog inland and bringing in some big surf. Summer was coming on fast and I needed a taste of nature.

If I hadn't been so involved with politics, I knew I'd be into something environmental. The first Earth Day had come and gone six weeks earlier in April. I hadn't paid much attention. It didn't have the same urgency as anti-racism and anti-war work. The other drawback was that environmentalists generally didn't see problems in terms of capitalism. The movement had an apolitical if not bourgeois ring to it. Still, some part of me—a very alienated part—felt more passionate about the survivability of the natural world than my own species. At some level our fates were intertwined, but I knew that ultimately we were dependent on Mother Nature, not the other way around. While we were messing up our natural world, I was sure that humans were much more at risk than the earth. At any rate, that morning in early June, I put down *The Origin of the Family, Private Property and the State* by Engels and headed to the beach.

Two surfers took off on their boards on the first big wave of the set. One dumped and the other flashed past me down the face. As I expected, the pregnant hump of the second wave in the set was forming outside, and I flicked my fins and took a few strokes out toward it. The waves were building up quickly, already a five or six-foot drop from the top to the base. If I went over the barrel without cutting a good angle down the face, I was headed for some serious time scrambled like a rag doll under water. The trick was timing. Trying to catch a wave early, especially in body surfing, meant missing it, and getting it too late meant it had already gained momentum and was controlling you. But knowing something and being able to execute it are two different things. I caught that watery thug too late to pull out, and found myself going over the falls straight into a maelstrom. The choice was a free-fall belly flop or to tuck and curl and hopefully flip out behind the chaotic whitewater as it rushed to the beach. The flip was obviously the preferred maneuver, unless the water was too shallow. I'd heard stories of broken necks suffered by attempting this graceful bit of escapism. I laughed at fate: The chance of that happening was even less than the likelihood that the FBI would show up at the office today. Besides, I knew we were near high tide, and that meant deeper water. With a quick spin, I popped out behind the wave. Giddy with adrenaline and a head rush, I was soon angling my way down another wave's shimmering face to the shore of our nerve-wracked nation.

Mike and I had added the footage from the police's attack on the LA Panthers and the collective revised the narration. But the changes made the call for armed revolution so explicit that it was clear to everyone that *Repression* had become far too radical to use as an organizing tool, even in a society as polarized as ours. The film was shelved. However, a song we had on the soundtrack continued to haunt me. It was by Elaine Brown, one of the leaders of the LA Panthers. Several times she repeated the line, *"We'll have to get guns and be men."* The lyric had begun to sound like a tragic fate rather than the call to arms it was meant to be. Elaine and others seemed to have dropped out of sight, and we heard that many of the Panthers had retreated to Oakland. It definitely felt like a certain phase of the revolution was over.

Judy and Jonathan had predicted that either the Panthers were going to be destroyed by continuing to promote armed struggle, or they were going to devolve into some sort of social democratic party. They couldn't survive as a guerilla army because, Jonathan added ominously, the kind of organization needed for that remained to be built. This brought up a whole range of questions.

The nonstop torrent of traumatic events that was 1968 had knocked the Democrat out of me. But it was one thing to stop believing in the system and another to find a replacement worth dying for. The Soviet Union was just another version of imperialist bully. Maoism was enticing, but even if Mao's excesses were forgiven, the Chinese experiment was taking place in an agrarian nation of peasants. The U.S. was an industrial behemoth that stretched around the globe. I was more and more convinced that capitalism was an inherently evil system as Marxists explained in a hundred different ways. But it seemed that students, middle-class intellectuals, and the poorest and most exploited in America were the only ones willing to take a chance on something new. The system was spinning out of control—but was the working class, especially the white part, ready to revolt?

Nixon and LBJ before him had demonstrated all too well that the American government had a multitude of ways of placating a good percentage of its citizens, no matter how grievous the sins and excesses of our system. Nixon had long shown he was a master at demonizing those who fought him. He'd red-baited political opponents in the 1950s, and he repeatedly said those against the war in Vietnam were weak-willed commie sympathizers—or, at a minimum, un-American. This tactic began to backfire on him, especially after the Cambodian invasion, because among the protestors was a distinctly patriotic group, the Vietnam Veterans Against the War (VVAW). They'd begun asking the obvious, yet heretical question: "In this war that even the President seems to admit is a mistake, which of us will be the last to die?" It seemed to me that these guys weren't even radical. They were simply the sanest among us asking to end the madness. Nixon, and others caught in his web of lies, had the gall to suggest that the VVAW were not really veterans but addicts, welfare cheats, and, of course, un-American. The soldiers, discharge papers in hand, begged to differ.

I was still going out with films, explaining the situation as if I had a handle on it. The student audiences were highly receptive, yet they were dispersing. After the Kent State shooting, many colleges stayed closed for the rest of the school year. As the summer of 1970 began, LA Newsreel's focus was blurry: Nothing was clear. Turmoil was the norm. The whole scene was taking on elements of a bad trip and made me very uptight.

Impulsively, I drove out to the desert and hiked a few miles up the narrow canyon above our cabin to a pool at the base of a sequence of five waterfalls. I dove into the frigid snowmelt, climbed onto a flat boulder, and flattened myself against the warm, speckled granite, worn smooth by millions of years of watery caresses. I returned, again, to the question of taking up arms. Was I ready to personally pick up the gun, or even to directly support those who were trying to bring the war home? Thus far, supporting the Panthers hadn't demanded a final answer to that because they weren't engaged in direct military actions. But they might be at any time, and now the Weathermen were going underground.

Where was that switch that turned one into a soldier and, if necessary, a killer?

Stanley's words echoed in my head. The thought that I didn't hate enough made me feel like a wimp. However, I harbored an unwelcome suspicion that if I'd been drafted, they would have been able to make me into a certain kind of man who could have killed. That was their specialty, and I'd met enough vets to accept that I wouldn't have been strong enough, man enough, to stand up to them, at least until I got my hands bloodied. That seemed to be the plight of lots of guys coming back from 'Nam.

Something FJ mentioned that night in Berkeley about organizing the returning vets came to mind: "Even if they thought we never should have been in Vietnam, what made the war memorable was their own guys, the guys they loved, not the guys they hated. The guys they were willing to die for made the war important, not the ones they were trying to kill."

There's a big difference between being willing to kill in the name of hate and being willing to die for someone you love. The most powerful and dangerous emotion was love, not hate. Love was dangerous because it inspired a person to believe things could be better. It powered a faith in the future and a willingness to die for it.

When I was younger I'd often pondered what I'd die for, and what always came to mind first was, I'd sacrifice myself to save my own kid. It was easy to imagine. I figured any father would die to save his child, to insure its future. That felt right and natural. But now I saw how that "natural" impulse underscored how wonderfully dangerous love was: More people had died and killed in its name that any other emotion. Che Guevara spoke about the revolutionary being motivated by great feelings of love. And even though I no longer believed in it as a religion, I dug that Christianity was based on the notion of Jesus dying for the love of mankind. For believers, his love gave humanity a future. Yet, while Christians loved that story, they had killed a lot of people in order to defend it. In spite of everything, love could turn into its opposite. Love was dangerous, then and now.

So, what did I love? The question morphed into whom did I love? I had to acknowledge, if only to myself, that love represented another kind of danger since meeting Stephanie. As a kid I believed that love was strong enough to hold people together. Then my parents' divorce ripped that faith out of me. Even fifteen years later, I didn't use the word "love," didn't trust the feeling or the "forever" fantasy that it invoked.

I didn't dare love, and I couldn't hate. Fuck me.

I leaned over and drank from the pool. The bright sunlight careened through the cottonwood leaves and flickered off the water. A movement rippled the water; a snake glided across the pool in a spreading *S* pattern, head held high. It was big, four or five feet, with a triangular head: a rattler. Tongue flicking like a magic wand, it appeared to be moving past me, yet the proximity of danger delivered an adrenaline rush and a memory.

I was sixteen years old, hunting with my friend Vic Pine, just a few miles downstream from this very pool, but past where the stream finally filtered beneath the desert floor. Crunching along the dry wash, I heard my name being called frantically. I came around a big smoke tree, and there was Vic sprawled flat on his belly, holding onto the stock of his .22 rifle while he pinned a writhing rattlesnake to the gravel with the barrel.

"Holy shit, man, what the hell are you doin'?"

"I was just trying to look at the son of a bitch, but I'm stuck."

"Well, let him go."

"I can't; he might come after me. Besides, let's catch him. We could sell it."

I looked at the snake. It was lunging every which way, unable to coil or escape. I looked at Vic. Obviously, "Let's catch him," meant, "Why don't you pick him up?"

It was crazy but the lure and thrill of danger trumped my fear. "Keep him pinned," I ordered.

"Don't worry about that," Vic replied.

I took my own .22 in my left hand and very deliberately shimmied the barrel along the snake's body until it pressed firmly an inch behind the snake's head. Then I reached across my body with my right hand, and got two fingers and my thumb close behind the head. As I slid the barrel away, the snake's mouth arched open and it tried to turn on me. I held on tightly and with my left hand I took hold of it near the tail. "Let him go!" I shouted to Vic.

Vic pulled the rifle off as I stood with the snake. Instantly it began to thrash and twist with surprising strength. I tried to hold it away from me, high in the air, but it felt like it was going to wriggle out of my grasp. My hands began to sweat and I worried my grip would slip. I squeezed harder, which only increased the snake's turmoil. The snake wrapped the last foot of its body that was free around my left wrist. I felt like I was being pulled into the snake, that I couldn't keep away from it. This brought the serpent closer to my face, and I ended up looking straight into its bulging eyes. While terrifying, this also showed me that my thumb and forefinger were solidly behind its head. As long as I held that position, I had control. I exhaled and instead of fighting the animal's movements I began to move with it, bending my wrists, elbows, and knees as the creature thrashed and strained. From that point on, as the snake flexed and arched, so did I. We were no longer in a fight, but rather, it was as though we were dancing. The snake continued writhing, but there was no longer the same desperation in the air. We were joined. We were in it together.

With a start, I came back and scanned the pool. There was no evidence of the rattler in the water, and I felt a jolt of fear, now vulnerable to the unseen. Then I noticed movement as it slithered behind a boulder on the far bank and I relaxed back into the sense memory of my *pas de deux* with the snake.

I was groovin' along with the snake, with Vic following as we came out of the shallow canyon where we'd been shooting. We walked across the desert to where a house was being built. A carpenter was dumbfounded to see us appear, but while cursing us as idiots, he managed to find a pillowcase in his truck that I dropped the critter into. Then Vic and I drove into town and sold it to the Japanese florist who considered rattlesnake meat a delicacy. I have no memory how in hell we'd known to do that, but it was a perfect ending to a wonderfully dangerous adventure.

I swam back to the shore and put on my shorts and boots. I had to admit that I was attracted to danger. Was that why I'd become so deeply involved in making revolution? Was the romance with danger and clear-cut, moral outrage the reason that so many middle-class kids like me were turning on this country to the point of violent rebellion? Had the combination of love and danger put me on the path to joining the Weathermen? I didn't have answers, but I was definitely dancing with the snake that was imperialist America run amok.

I was also dancing with the snake known as communism. The basic attraction was easy to understand: from each according to his ability, to each according to his need. It was as American as communal barn building, forming a posse to catch bad guys, or Medicare, which had started just four years earlier. Or welfare; my mom had helped start the Welfare and Friendly Aid Society in Palm Springs when I was a boy. It always made sense to me that those better off should help out those in need. Our country was full of socialistic practices, only we called it the American way. But it seemed that most Americans distrusted communism, and it usually had to do with two things: God and freedom. Commies were notorious atheists. I don't know when I learned that God and religious practice were not allowed in the USSR and China, but the lesson came early and often. It wasn't ranted about—people didn't rant in my house—but I knew I should pray for those kept away from God.

However, after an All-Powerful God had let me down as a kid, I didn't care much about protecting religions. But I did think people should be free to make their own choices. Freedom—that was the big issue America was built on: freedom of religion, freedom to own land, freedom to own a gun, and freedom from others telling you what to do without any recourse. But freedom didn't mean much if people weren't treated equally. Racism was real, and improving civil rights had come too little, too late.

Yes, the government sometimes looked like it was trying to change, but it seemed like the more they promised the worse it got. The string of lies about winning the war in Vietnam proved that. And even if you thought that elections were run fairly—which Nixon had put into question—what difference did it make if your candidate was assassinated? It wasn't lost on anyone that our own Declaration of Independence encouraged us to overthrow the government should we, once again, find evidence of an effort to place us under "absolute Despotism."

I was convinced of the need for revolution, and I accepted it was going to have to be violent. The question was how to go about it, and what to replace this system with. Communists seemed to come in all shades of red, but Lenin was evidently the man to listen to after Marx had explained the inherent shortcomings of capitalism. Lenin said there had to be a revolutionary party, and the road to socialism must be led by the most conscious elements of the working class. That was seductive to be sure since I liked to think I was nothing if not conscious. Working class was a trickier question. I'd been a student most of my life, but I'd worked every summer, including a few digging ditches. I wasn't getting paid for what I was doing now, but I was working hard.

Whatever I was, socialism promised economic fairness. Individuals could become truly free. Mao took it a step further, into spiritual transformation. He said that individual needs and identity had to be channeled to the point of total immersion in the collective. The result was to be the creation of a social utopia that had an intoxicating mystical quality. It was far out, but it wasn't that hard to imagine or believe in. After all, I'd once believed that humans had suddenly appeared in the Garden of Eden and were going to Heaven. On top of that, I'd experienced the oneness of life through LSD and mescaline.

Communism shuffled all this together right here on earth. Since I'd put painting aside, I had begun to work collectively. I felt I'd accomplished far more than I could have ever done alone. It gave me hope. Not that it was easy. You had to be disciplined: Study, work hard, and commit to a higher good. It seemed clear that some collective authority had to run the revolutionary effort.

This brought up Joe Stalin. Jonathan in Newsreel was a fan of the man, as were many Americans during World War II when the Russian communists were in alliance with the United States and the rest of the Allies. But after the Russians crushed the Nazis' advance into Russia and the war ended, my friend Jonathan pointed out that Americans had been brainwashed to turn on Stalin. It was in the nature of capitalism to attack socialism, just like Marx said, even if it wasn't in the interest of the common man. Stalin definitely got some bad press, and the whole socialist experiment in the USSR was pretty well discredited by the time I was being radicalized. Certainly Mike had no good words for him. But Jonathan thought that Uncle Joe's ideas about leading the way from socialism to communism were right on, even when it involved purging and killing his fellow Russians. Yes, he argued, the socialist path had been violent, but it was because it had to be tough and united to stand up to the Cold War onslaught from capitalist countries. Imagine, Jonathan asked, how much easier and kinder the road to collective bliss would be if America were socialist as well. I could imagine it. I wanted to believe he was right, but it required a leap of faith right up there with believing in Heaven and the virgin birth.

I returned from the desert knowing I needed to get away from students, revolutionaries, and political analysis, and back into the everyday world. I didn't want to disappear into wilderness. I wanted to go through the country again and take the pulse: I imagined a longer version of last summer's excursion with Stef. I asked her if she wanted to take off for a whole month. I wasn't sure she'd go, since she'd been teaching in a nursery school, but the lure of the road—or was it me?—was too strong.

We were discussing it one evening when Bill dropped by my place to get stoned. "We're talking about taking a trip around the country. I want to go through the South to the East Coast," I said.

"You're looking pretty shaggy. You're not worried about crackers and another *Easy Rider*?" he asked.

I shrugged and said, "I'll cut my hair and beard to be safe."

"I'm not ready to go all that way on a motorcycle," Stef said.

"Seems to me a vacation is a bourgeois luxury," Bill said.

It was hard to know if he was being serious, but Stef nailed him anyway. "I've been reading *Reminiscences of Lenin* by Krupskaya, his wife, and she talks about how she and Vladimir got away for six weeks into the mountains to read and write in the year before the Russian Revolution." She added, "I think vacations are a proletarian invention, because they work so hard."

"Right on, comrade!" I cheered.

Bill laughed, "Well, I'm convinced. And since you're going in the van, will you drop me off in New York? I should get back and see my mother."

"No," Stef and I said at the same time. We looked at one another with similar smiles. More and more we were in sync, making decisions that were filled with unspoken agreements and common cause.

"Okay," Bill said, "I guess being lovebirds isn't counter-revolutionary either." He sighed. "I'm giving the revolution a few more months to get going, or I'm going to become a monk or a nomad or..."

"Are there communist nomads?" I kidded.

"Life would be one long traveling meeting." Stef laughed.

"I guess it wouldn't be too different from now," Bill said seriously. "I'm fed up with this study group. It's like politics is my girlfriend."

"You need to get laid," Stef said. He looked at her with wishful eyes and she added, "No, Bill," and disappeared into the kitchen to make dinner.

"But, comrade," he pleaded, and shook his head in mock despair. "It's never that simple."

"Nomad is an island," I intoned.

Bill groaned at my pun, then called to Stef, "I hear there's a women's meeting tonight. Aren't you going to be late?"

"Only after she finishes the dishes," I joked. I was pretty sure I wasn't a male chauvinist since I did a lot of the cooking.

Stef came back into the living room, licking spaghetti sauce from a wooden spoon. "I don't know," she admitted. "I'm not sure I need reminders about what it means to be a woman in a man's world."

"Man's world," Bill snorted. "Women don't get that it only looks that way."

Stef looked at me to see if I agreed with him. I shrugged and nodded.

"That's the problem, right there. You guys need to go to this meeting more than me. You're clueless and sexist."

I started to disagree until I saw that she had begun to sob.

"What's wrong?" I asked, totally baffled.

It took a moment, but she finally answered, "I'm in love with you, that's what's wrong."

It was the first time she'd said that word and I was stunned. My mind was flooded by a staggering array of thoughts and feelings until I realized that I couldn't return the word even if I felt the same way. And I had no idea why she was crying. In the strained silence that followed, Bill mumbled something and scooted out the front door.

"I—I...that's...but why are you crying?" I finally asked.

"Because I'm as confused as you are," she said, dabbing at her runaway eyeliner, "...almost."

I stepped forward and she accepted a hug. Then she kissed me and went to her purse. "I'm going to that group," she said.

I looked at her with questioning eyes.

"I'm not mad. I just need to think and be with other women for a while."

"Are you coming back tonight?" I asked.

She shook her head no.

"Ever?"

"Yes, Vladimir, I'd never pass up a revolutionary vacation with you." She pulled her long black hair into a ponytail, flashed me that warm, sexy smile of hers, and was out the door with the reminder, "Don't forget the spaghetti sauce on the stove."

Love. I poured myself a glass of wine, put "A Love Supreme" on the turntable, and sat down to see if John Coltrane could explain what was going on. I'd often gone to hear him in New York, and he always had something to say to me. Now, he didn't disappoint, but what he revealed with his quartet's insistent yet sublime cascade of sound was that emotion and spirit overwhelm us mere humans. I wasn't only scarred by my parents' divorce to the point of not trusting love; love itself was scary, no more predictable than it was resistible.

I leaned back into the couch. At the last Newsreel meeting, Christine had declared, "The personal is political." It looped into Coltrane's sonic prayer, repeating over and over like a mantra.

17

OTHER REVOLUTIONS

The South was a different country. It wasn't just the Spanish moss and the myriad of greens that greeted our eyes as we drove through Louisiana. It was more than the symphony of bugs and the muggy, thick air that put curls in Stef's hair. It was more than kudzu growing everywhere, the rich, comforting food, and the Southerners' hypnotic way of massaging the English language. Judging from walking around Meridian, Mississippi, they did racism differently. For one thing, compared to California the races lived side by side. In the neighborhood where we stayed with Mrs. Houze and her three grandkids, black and white folks seemed to cross paths a dozen times a day. The two races shopped in the same stores, swapped stories, and seemed to abide if not actually enjoy one another at a level rarely seen in Los Angeles. It seemed to me that prejudice played out differently in a shared space, when races grew up in close proximity. Racism was more upfront in the South. It couldn't be denied as it was in California. We had arrived in the South a few short years after segregation had been directly confronted, its legal basis partially destroyed. That didn't mean it wasn't still ingrained, but it no longer was an unchallenged way of life.

Elinor, our Newsreel comrade, had been a "freedom rider" back in 1963, and Mrs. Houze had put her up. When Elinor wrote her, Mrs. Houze had graciously invited us to visit and park our van in her driveway. When we showed up she whipped up a platter of the tastiest fried chicken I'd ever eaten. I was on my third piece when I asked if we could take her and her grandkids to the movie downtown. The three kids squealed. She looked at us and couldn't help shaking her head in wonder. "Lord, Lord; my, my, my," she said. "Well, the children are thrilled, but I'm afraid it would be too much for me."

I asked why.

"Movie theater only began to let Negroes sit downstairs two years ago. 'Fore that we had to sit in the balcony, if we got in at all." She patted her neck and forehead with a kerchief in the humid evening air. "When your friend Elinor came through with the others in 1963, I could hardly dream of this day. She was one brave little white girl." She turned to the eldest child. "Ella Mae, you clear the table with your brothers 'fore you go." Stef got up with the kids despite Mrs. Houze's protest and helped with the cleanup.

"'Brave' was how Elinor described you, Mrs. Houze," I said.

Mrs. Houze nodded modestly, but added, "We had to be, but each race made the other more brave. Down here, when it came time to stand up and say 'No more,' many black folks did something to make it happen. And the young ones took the most risks. But seeing others who weren't even black come from so far away to help...well, it did something good for your soul, made you even stronger."

She sent us off and soon Stef and I were sitting with three black kids who'd never been out of Meridian, Mississippi, watching Neil Simon's *The Out-of-Towners*. It was bizarre to watch the story of a Midwestern couple suffering a disastrous trip to New York through the eyes of these youngsters as they enjoyed popcorn and air-conditioning in that theater for the first time in their lives. Stef and I agreed that it felt at least as radical as showing Newsreel films.

In spite of the fun we had with the kids and the fresh berry pie Mrs. Houze fed us when we got back, I had a troubled sleep in our van that night. We were experiencing desegregation and racial integration that were the result of a civil rights movement that deeply believed in forcing the system to work as intended. Dr. King and millions of others were convinced that the white world could and would learn to share fairly. And—though begrudgingly, as evident from some stares and looks of displeasure we received going into the theater with the kids—white Southerners seemed to be making an effort to stay on the train to real equality that had been derailed after the abolition of slavery. The atmosphere was flush with hope as well as trepidation, but it was clear that folks like Mrs. Houze, having come so far and achieved so much, would keep on pressing.

The irony was that so many in the north, me included, had given up on the system in the process of confronting it. We'd moved the goal from integration to revolution. The Black Panther Party and many other Marxist groups considered the black population to be a scattered colony that had to overthrow, as Eldridge Cleaver called it, "the mother country." The particular communist party we were studying with, the California Communist League (CCL), took it all a step further. The CCL insisted that the black people in the South constituted a separate nation. After the coming revolution southern blacks would determine how they wanted to run things down there. Now that we were "down there," that notion seemed suspect if only because it seemed so far removed from the vision of Mrs. Houze, Dr. King, and the millions of others who had already made a monumental effort to integrate into and benefit from white society.

The next morning, I asked Mrs. Houze if she thought that black people would ever be in control in the South. She allowed as how that had been an idea people talked about in the 1930s, when blacks were a majority in Mississippi and Alabama, but after the war, when so many migrated north, the notion died out. "Now that we got the vote, I reckon we'll be sharing control. Thing is, we don't want to treat the white folks how they treated us. That's not good for anybody."

The South really was different if only because something radical had already happened. People who had never voted were voting. Laws and the face of government and law enforcement were being transformed. The times, they were a changing.

"Seems like the South is having both a political and cultural revolution," I said.

"We're moving toward justice," she nodded. "Thank the Lord."

Stef turned to me. "If hippies and everyone in the Cultural Revolution dropped back in, they could change the system too."

"Not likely," I replied. "They'd have to have the patience and iron will that black Southerners have, to say nothing of holding onto their own radical visions of peace and equality. It's too easy to be bought off."

Mrs. Houze listened and added, "It's true we had nowhere to go but up." She chuckled. "And I'm not talking 'bout Heaven."

In Tuskegee, Alabama, we stopped to see friends who'd just begun labor organizing. They were settling down to become a part of the New South, something they were convinced was emerging.

We drawled our way through Georgia. At a country store the friendly proprietor gave us some cornbread and sold us the ingredients for her recipe for black-eyed peas and ham hocks to cook in our camper. We pulled over and slept wherever we landed. Over and over we kept coming back to the question of whose revolution was it and where was it heading? Was the civil rights movement about making a capitalistic America more democratic, or was it a step toward socialism?

Russia had had a moderate revolution in 1906 that got rid of the tsar. Then it was followed in 1917 by the far more radical Bolshevik revolution. Those ardent Marxists rejected small changes and successfully instituted socialism. The state took over everything. Yet within a decade, a dictatorial proletarian leader was killing dissenters. Jonathan always insisted that Stalin's actions were made necessary because of attacks by the capitalist countries, but the old saying, "Power corrupts, and absolute power corrupts absolutely," rang in my head. Powerful changes were already happening here in the South. Would they be enough or simply the prelude to a far more radical change? Pressing questions kept me awake and, despite the heat, I felt a chill.

We reached the Atlantic at Cape Hatteras and headed up the East Coast. Before turning west, we drove all the way to Little Deer Island in Maine, where we picked blueberries and drank wine with friends of Stef's. As we traveled we found ourselves watching a lot more TV, something we rarely did since neither one of us owned one. But for weeks we caught up on the vision of the world being mirrored back to most Americans. We watched the turmoil and conflict that dominated network news at restaurants and during the few nights we spent in a motel. Something that looked a lot like revolution was being televised: The increasingly successful fight by the North Vietnamese against the most powerful imperialist country came to us nightly. And, despite government efforts to intimidate the networks, demonstrations featuring burning draft cards and sometimes burning bras were there for the curious to observe from their couches. The regional news found on TV or down at the corner drugstore in the local newspaper might mention a boy who'd been killed in Vietnam alongside news of a bombing by some radical group. Neither item of news was rare.

It was also easy to find the Cultural Revolution, and it wasn't hard to see how it was being co-opted. Americans had emerged from the 1950s both loving and hating their predictable, deadening consumer culture. To make this culmination of capitalism more appealing, the Cultural Revolution was being caricatured and sold back to America. "Psychedelic" and "Mod" became lifestyles and something to enjoy on *Laugh-In* and other popular TV shows. The result was often wildly funny, but behind the screen was a system that manufactured desire for things that the counterculture had originally opposed. As more and more of the population adopted alternative attitudes, dress, and values, "radical" and "hippie" were no longer daring personal and political statements; they had become lifestyles. And lifestyles could be changed as easily as buying a new car.

"Hippie" had died like the Diggers declared in 1967, but that cultural phenomenon had been reincarnated as the kids next door. Drugs and communes had once been "far out." Now they were "in."

As had happened to so much of black culture, the counterculture's rejection of the status quo was appropriated to sell product. It was similar to how Nixon and other politicians usurped radical political slogans. "Power to the people" was now a call for less government rather than a new form of government.

As disgusted as I was, I had to marvel at the way that capitalism marketed itself. It was able to make this system seem a necessary and inevitable part of life. Marketing was its favorite and most successful tool, propaganda at its most sublime. Through advertising, it both created and satisfied needs and desires. Marketing existed to make a profit on the human condition. That was its nature, both why and how it survived. I began to think of marketing as a virus, a disease that began as benign but was potentially devastating, with no known vaccine.

The Marxist in me despaired, but my Social Democrat was feeling upbeat. After all, lots of people realized that the current system was corrupt and unfair even though most of them still thought that the problem wasn't capitalism and its devil spawn, the modern corporation that lived only to make a profit. Many believed that we could make this system work for everyone, and, to be sure, political and cultural changes were happening across the land. You could still imagine that it was just a matter of time and that a revolution was happening without communist leadership. Maybe Mike's more optimistic predictions were right; it might be somewhat violent, but a new system would unfold organically until the opposition melted away. I could almost take the trip until I recalled that King and Bobby, our nonviolent Gandhis, had been assassinated, and no one had stepped up to take their places.

One night on the high plains of Oklahoma, we camped among a cluster of oaks not far off the highway. We awoke early the next morning, hungry and out of coffee. We drove into a small town and parked in front of the dusty windows of a secondhand store. It looked closed. I wandered down the street, convinced there must be a cafe somewhere. Stef called and waved to me as she disappeared inside the store. I found her searching the overloaded shelves and tables for abandoned treasure. We walked dreamily through the detritus of other lives, stories beckoning from every shelf. I sidled up next to her as she examined a child's cup. The long, painted handle was a giraffe's neck that worked as a straw when you sucked the top of the giraffe's head. At the bottom of the cup was painted, "That's a good girl."

"We gotta get that," I said without really knowing why. Stef gave me a surprised smile when we heard a sleepy, hoarse voice.

"Goodness gracious, you startled me." A plump, older woman in a wrinkled dress and uncombed hair stood blinking at us from down the aisle. "We're not really open, but I guess I left the door unlocked last night. It doesn't make much difference, 'cause stuff is already so cheap it hardly makes sense for anyone to steal it. What'd you find?"

Stef showed her the cup. The woman scratched her hip, smiled, and asked, "You folks got a little one?"

"No," Stef said, and we couldn't stifle self-conscious grins.

"Well, maybe this'll help things along. Anyway, it'll only set you back a quarter." We followed her back to an antique cash register to find some change for my dollar. We asked about what it was like living in a small town, and she inquired where we were going and where we'd been. Mrs. Maguire was intrigued and a bit tickled as this dark-haired beauty described the sights she'd seen with her shaggy companion. We had no rings on and she never asked if we were married, but as each casual piece of information gathered around us, it felt more and more like we were a couple.

There's something about being out of one's daily routine. Maybe it's that when we meet someone new, we have an opportunity to describe ourselves in a whole different way. It's not necessarily a lie; it's more like a new outfit that we try on to see how it fits. In this case, my new identity didn't have anything to do with politics or any opinions about the world in general. I simply was no longer a lone entity; I was morphing into "we" as Stef and I responded to questions from this friendly, curious, and—as evident in the stickers on a cabinet behind her—patriotic, Nixon-loving Republican. As we left she added, "It's the best part of running this place, seeing who shows up to claim what."

We drove twelve hours straight to Denver and camped in my sister's driveway that night, long after they'd gone to sleep. Jeanie's big family reflected her adherence to the Catholic faith we'd been raised with. She was the only remaining Catholic among my family, but she was cool; family was more important to her than religious judgments. May her God bless her forever. Like Jimmy and Gail, my other siblings, Jeanie was more a product of the 1950s than the 60s. They'd all graduated from college before JFK was even elected, and any rules they'd broken involved cigarettes and liquor. They were good people, but they were from a different generation.

The next morning my nieces and nephews, two, six, eight, and ten, crowded into our camper van, bouncing on the bed and peering into the cupboards. Stef and I were exotic, the black-sheep uncle and his beautiful Jewish girlfriend driving around the country…and we weren't even married!

Later that day, with Jeanie's blessing, we took two-year-old Alex and drove to Boulder to drop off some films for a SDS-sponsored screening. We found a playground, romped about for a while, and put him down for a nap on our bed.

We didn't know the people who were renting the films or which version of SDS they represented, not that it mattered. Marge and Wilson turned out to be veterans of Chicago and quite committed to the Weatherman philosophy. Marge was edgy, small with intense black eyes. She wound her mahogany-colored hair around her finger as she spoke, which she did much of the time. In less than a minute, she moved the conversation from casual chitchat to her politics. "Lots of people today realize that you can't use sex as a way to control another person. We say 'smash monogamy,' but this isn't just some hippie thing. This is the basis for a whole different kind of society."

Wilson—her partner, her main squeeze, definitely not her husband—sang in a Harry-Belafonte-style calypso, "House built on a weak foundation will not stand, oh no. Story's told through all creation, will not stand, oh no." He laughed and took a drag off his cigarette.

She ignored him. "It's been clear to us since we met in '67 that to build our relationship on an institution based on the ownership of a woman is the antithesis of love. Marriage is a bourgeois institution."

"Are you going to have any children?" Stef asked.

Marge blinked rapidly. "We gave up our boy to a beautiful couple in Iowa. They support what we're doing and," she paused, "they couldn't have kids and wanted one more than anything." She twisted her hair.

"Children are everyone's responsibility," Wilson broke in. "Maternity doesn't mean control...I mean, almost anyone can care for a child if that's their thing."

"Far out," I managed to say.

Wilson added, "Some people have a hard time understanding this, but it wouldn't be safe for Donny to have him with us while we, you know, do what has to be done to get rid of this fascist government."

"What about you guys?" Marge asked.

We looked at one another, suddenly self-conscious. "I don't know what we're going to do...but I'm definitely not into marriage," I said.

"You can't get an insurance policy on a relationship, and that's what marriage tries to be," Stef added.

"After the revolution, after we make a world that's safe and welcoming to children, they promised us we could get to know the boy, you know, like an aunt and uncle or something like that," Wilson explained further.

"Still, that must have been hard," Stef said quietly.

Marge inhaled, effectively damming the tears that had filled her eyes. "Not as hard as watching children slowly starving to death."

"Marge saw some shit in the Peace Corp, in Kenya," Wilson added.

"But it could have been in Guatemala or a child killed by napalm in 'Nam," she broke in. "It's all the result of the same heartless killing machine that's got to be stopped."

"Right on," I said, immediately unsure if I meant to be encouraging them. "So here are the films for your screening tonight: *Off the Pig* and *San Francisco State*. Just mail them back to the address on the film can." I pointed to my van. "We gotta split. We took my sister's two-year-old for the day, and he just crashed out into a nap before we pulled up. I want to drive back to Denver while he's still asleep."

"Oh, can I see him?" Marge burst out.

They followed us and peered at Alex zonked out in the back of the van. "He's a doll," Marge said.

"Youngest of four," I replied. "My sister's really into it."

Wilson smiled. "That's cool. Somebody's got to raise the consciousness of the next generation."

"I understand not everyone can do what we're doing," Marge spilled out. "You have to commit all the way." She studied the address on the film can. "Los Angeles. Did you make these films?"

"Not those. We did one on the LA Panthers, but the pigs sorta wiped them out before we finished it."

Marge's voice asked quietly, "If we had to get out of here in a hurry, you know, how would you feel about us 'visiting' you in LA?"

I saw fear flash across Stef's eyes and felt my own stomach knot. I looked back at Marge and took a big, leisurely breath, giving myself time to think. "It's possible," I said, "but you should know that the FBI recently showed up unannounced, and the local cops have been known to keep a watch on the office and who knows where else." Then I added, "They tend to take these films personally."

"Fuck!" Marge swore. "Of course they would."

Stef and I were silent as we drove back to Denver. "They're like soldiers for a radical hippie army," I finally said, "ready to give up everything and die for the promise of something better."

"They may be soldiers, but I've yet to see an army," Stef said. "They're crazy," she spat out, "and when I think of their little boy, I feel sick."

A day later we headed home through the Rockies and found ourselves pulled like nesting birds into a vast mountainside of shimmering gold and orange, interspersed with dashes of blood red and yellow. After walking about in awe, I whispered into Stef's ear, "The most mind-blowing thing about an aspen grove is that it's a model of communism."

Stef turned to me as if I were nuts. She scooped up a handful of leaves and lofted them over me.

"It's true," I laughed. "It's the largest single organism on earth. Under the ground, every tree is interconnected, part of the whole. They don't look it, but all these individual trees are really one big tree."

Stef grabbed me as the leaves floated all around us. "I love you," she said, and this time she didn't rush off to a women's meeting like she did the first time she uttered those words.

I was seized by an exquisite discomfort. For the first time in my life, I was sure I felt the same, but I couldn't say it. She looked at me with her dark, daring eyes. I didn't want to hurt this woman. What choice did I have but to tell her the truth? "I...I don't trust that word," I stammered. "So I don't use it."

She peered at me and asked, "Your parents' divorce?"

I felt such relief I almost cried. Instead, I kissed her and said, "The thing is, I feel like I'm ready to have a child."

She nodded, "I know what you mean. I'm ready too."

"But I'm not interested in getting married. I don't believe in..."

"Me either," she interrupted.

"I don't see how anybody can pretend to see their whole life into the future. I mean...I feel like I can commit to the next two years, but who knows what the hell is going to happen beyond that."

She leaned away a bit. "Just two years?"

"It's not that I want to be together for only two years. It's just that I can't see clearly further than that. I don't want to lie to you and pretend I can."

She looked into my eyes for a long time, then looped her arm through mine to walk back to our trusty VW van. "I think I can live with that."

Soon, Stef stopped using the pill, and we enthusiastically set about trying to have a child.

Film screenings picked up as schools reopened. We encouraged the budding student activists to protest the war and effect change on their campuses. It didn't seem like enough.

Our new office was only a few blocks from the burnt-out Panther headquarters. The Panthers themselves were not much in evidence in Los Angeles. At some point we'd shown the re-cut version of the film to a few of them; they hadn't liked the changes. Soon after, they borrowed one of our two sixteen-millimeter film projectors for a screening and refused to return it. They said they'd lost it, but we knew they had "liberated" it. We argued but it was a lost cause, payback of sorts and a further reminder that the alliance both groups had once worked so hard to maintain was now unraveling.

The Marxist study group was going full steam. Each week a different member would lead the discussion on a work we were reading. When it was Stef's turn, she chose to discuss Mao's *Talks at the Yenan Forum on Art and Literature*. She had been an artist since she was little and wanted to understand how best to apply her particular skills, insights, and passions to our revolutionary movement. She had brought in several Chinese children's books to the nursery school where she worked, but she was wary of the rigid "Socialist Realism" style that marked Soviet and revolutionary Chinese art. I knew she was nervous, but I figured it was her usual intimidation around Judy and Jonathan when it came to political theory.

She began by pointing out that Mao had written that artists and writers must live among the masses and "create a variety of characters out of real life and help the masses to propel history forward… and produce works which awaken the masses, fire them with enthusiasm, and impel them to unite and struggle to transform their environment." That, she pointed out, wasn't too different from what we'd been doing in Newsreel. However, Mao insisted that the only worthwhile art was art that supported the masses and their revolution. He was adamant that the Communist Party was the final arbiter of what constituted art, and he had no use for work that reflected the individual or the unconscious. It was clear that he considered individual expression to be bourgeois or worse, a counterrevolutionary tendency. Stef made it clear that she had no problem with striving to understand and honor the working-class perspective, but to argue that it was the only valid form of creative expression was, in her eyes, ridiculous. Mao, she insisted with impressive resolve, was full of it. He was dictatorial and didn't respect or understand the creative process. In the edgy discussion that followed, several people argued that overcoming the practical problems of waging a successful revolution was far more important than the theoretical repression of individual expression. By the end, it was clear that most of LA Newsreel was committed to the chairman's position. They thought Stef had fallen victim to petit-bourgeois individualism and that we needed to have another "Criticism and Self-Criticism" session, a Maoist tool to stop backsliding and keep the comrades on track. C and S-C was scheduled for the next meeting.

During the meeting I hadn't said much, and Stef had avoided looking at me. As usual, it took me a while to understand what I was feeling. Once we were alone, I said that her challenging Mao both thrilled me and freaked me out. I agreed with her that the best art came from encouraging creativity in individuals. Creativity that was shackled to an ideology or a particular group was bound to become stilted and predictable. As she'd said, this was true of socialist realism, but, I added, it had also happened to classical and religious art in Europe during the nineteenth century. On the other hand, even before I became a Marxist, the events of 1968 had convinced me to put aside my painting to help bring about social and political change. If adhering to a collective vision was what was necessary for a political revolution to succeed, then it was a small personal sacrifice for the good of the many. But that was a big "if."

Stef was a kaleidoscope of conflicting emotions. She said she hadn't thought that her opinion about art might lead to her leaving Newsreel, but now that seemed like a real possibility. She was scared and excited, but not guilty. No way was she going through a C and S-C session. However, she admitted through tears, she was terrified that this could mean the end of us. Finally, with her eyes reflecting a trembling joy, she told me that she was pregnant.

18

A BOUGEOIS INSTITUTION

The personal and the political had been thoroughly shuffled, and I'd been dealt a hell of a hand. I had a woman toward whom I had taboo "L" word feelings, a baby on the way, and a cause and organization I was committed to. Could I have it all? As I struggled to sort it out, the problem was resolved in a most unpredictable manner; everyone involved with Los Angeles Newsreel decided to dissolve the organization itself. It was unanimous. We all agreed that we could no longer ignore the changes in the political environment. Working to stop the war and radicalize students and everyday citizens wasn't enough. The material conditions demanded a radical turn for a radical organization. Strangely enough, the timing of the decision had nothing to do with art or Stef's position. We had sidestepped the issue of our future as a group until it pushed its way to the top of the agenda.

I was sad and I was relieved. Los Angeles Newsreel had been the soil for the creation of a new me. My reincarnation was empowered to confront a society that drove me crazy as well as made me care enough to want to change it. Making and distributing documentaries collectively had been deeply challenging as well as satisfying. But it was also like an affair that was too full of contradictions to last. It made it easier that my comrades—those supportive, passionate, and irritating friends—ultimately agreed that our collective work had come to an end. That is, unless we each joined a communist party. That was a very different proposition.

While the level of commitment to a Marxist party or ideology varied among us, LA Newsreel had always studied with a few CCL members. After a study group we would often pass out leaflets supporting that hardline organization in Echo Park, the working-class Latino neighborhood where we met. The responses were rarely encouraging and made it even clearer that joining a party was a serious commitment. In addition, it went without saying that it was something the FBI would want to know. Unusual for our collective, joining became an individual, secret decision, though it wasn't hard to guess who had decided what.

I was convinced that the American system was rotten to the core. But I was unconvinced that taking orders from a political organization with leaders I barely knew was the right way to go. I needed to believe that this party could lead us out of the mess we were in without creating an even bigger mess. I'd already had an experience where high priests and an absolute boss controlled my fate. That hadn't turned out well.

It was obvious that both America and the Soviet Union had come to power using great violence internally: Communist governments in the USSR and China had slaughtered their dissidents while America's early economy rested upon slavery and we had wiped out many of the Native Americans. Both systems were soaked in blood, yet the dream of providing a voice and justice for the common man was found in both socialism and American democracy. However, they went at it differently. Under a communist party in America, there would be no attempt at democracy, at least initially. I would be putting my trust in a "dictatorship of the proletariat." As much as I distrusted the electoral process in the USA, was I ready to say it always had to be a sham?

There was another thing, although I didn't like to admit it: The meetings and endless discussions about abstract political theory bored the idealism out of me.

Stef felt the same way for another reason. The blacklist that had destroyed her parents' careers had knocked any card-carrying communist inclinations out of her. She didn't know for sure if her dad was ever a party member, but she was proud that he had refused to name other potential party members and risked going to jail. He had sacrificed his career to uphold the constitutional right to not have to tell the government if he had joined a political organization. He upheld the Fifth Amendment while our government, through Senator McCarthy and the House Un-American Activities Committee, had tried to destroy various constitutional rights in the name of saving them. But she did know that her father and many progressive people from the 1950s found the American Communist Party no longer worthy of support. She had watched this unfold as an eight-year-old, and now she was understandably wary of getting involved with any communist group.

A crazy paradox had come home to roost: We were convinced that the country was being run unconstitutionally. But was the best alternative to try to overthrow this government and replace it with a political organization that reserved the option of taking away rights? I knew what my friend Jonathan would say: Our freedom was an illusion. Our generation was dying for a war we didn't want; minorities were still second-class citizens even one hundred years after a war that promised equality; and the system was rigged in favor of the rich and white.

The bottom line was that I agreed with my Newsreel comrades that the system was corrupt and shared the desire to take our efforts to another level. Whether one joined a communist party or not, the path was clear. The time had come to focus our ideas and visions of the future on the industrial working class, to learn from, influence, and hopefully raise the consciousness of the proletariat.

First, though, Stef and I announced the joyous news to our families: "We're having a baby! And, by the way, we're not getting married." Her parents and my dad and stepmother were excited for us. Their liberal open-mindedness was being stretched, but they were delicate in their questioning of our decision not to marry and soon were enthusiastically planning parties to celebrate our anti-bourgeois union. However, our bubble of euphoria immediately burst when we told my mother and Paul.

"Are you crazy?" he yelled at me. "The kid will be a bastard, and you won't have any legal rights to it." He turned to Stef and added, "And you could be stuck with all the financial responsibility if the two of you split up."

Stef left the room sobbing, followed by my mother trying to comfort her. I fumed while Paul busied himself with lighting a cigar. We sat there, polarized as usual, abandoned by the women, in uncomfortable silence. After a few puffs, he softened his tone but not his message. Yes, he thought I was an idiot, but he insisted he was only trying to save me further grief. Basically, he admitted, he was happy for me. He thought having a kid would make me grow up and become more realistic. I didn't want to ruin his day by telling him I was going to work in some factory and prepare for the socialist takeover of the United States. Yet.

Still, by the time we left, I'd been convinced that as square as marriage was, there were some good reasons for it legally. Nonetheless, we wanted to do it our way and soon began planning to elope.

In November of 1970, for the first time in six years of war, there were no American combat fatalities reported for an entire week. Nixon argued that the war effort was slowing down and vehemently attacked Democrats, hippies, and anti-war demonstrators. However, the anguish over 40,000 Americans who had already died fighting in that distant land was still vivid, as was the awareness that an estimated 400,000 Vietnamese had also died. The senseless killing of so many innocent civilians was hardly offset by the trial of Army Lt. William Calley on November 17, for leading a massacre of villagers in the Vietnamese hamlet of M Lai. Most Americans wanted the war over and the midterm election results were a big disappointment for Republicans.

Yet the president kept dragging on this crusade, searching in vain for "an honorable peace," an unlikely ending to what more and more Americans saw as a dishonorable war.

Adding to the gloom were the deaths of two of the most spectacular, soulful performers of our age, Janis Joplin and Jimi Hendrix. They had lit up the 60s like shooting stars since the Monterrey Pop Festival and then died within two weeks of one another. Drugs were blamed for both deaths, but then again, drugs were being blamed for damn near everything. On the other hand, the best-selling paperback for the year was *The Greening of America*, which declared that a New Consciousness was changing the culture and our very country from the inside out. America, it claimed, looked like a Love-In in many ways and, as it matured, would evolve into a beautiful, liberated society. It was true that the events of the 60s had seen millions of my generation through enormous personal changes both painful and ecstatic. I had morphed from a faltering Catholic, apolitical Republican kid into a nature-loving Marxist with Buddhist tendencies.

But, it wasn't enough that that my generation was transforming our society in many ways. In spite of ongoing, mass protests, the U.S. was still bombing civilians in Vietnam, Laos, and Cambodia. Our country remained in the grip of a lying, manipulative president; he may have been mad, but he was also a brilliant politician. Mike joked that our only hope for returning to a bit of peace and sanity was for Richard Nixon to self-destruct. That seemed as likely as electing a socialist. A political revolution was nowhere to be seen on the horizon and the Cultural Revolution and peace movement had shown their limitations. My LA Newsreel comrades—now ex-Newsreel—weren't betting on the hippie revolution any more than on the Weathermen or Black Panthers. So we found jobs in the major industries with the hopes of connecting with like-minded souls and developing a vanguard among the working class. Whether this would lead to taking over our government from the lying politicians and wealthy warlords was the big unknown.

By the end of November, Stef had a job at the phone company. She lasted only a few months before being fired for trying to organize her information operators into a union. I told her she went out with class, "working class." I got my hair sheared at a barber school, lied about my education and was hired at the General Motors plant in South Gate on the other side of Watts. I landed on the assembly line, getting Buicks and Chevys ready for their paint jobs. My partner working the other side of the car was a biker who was usually stoned on reds and other paranoia-inducing downers. He spent the first month convinced I was a cop or FBI agent because I looked so goddamn straight. It was crazy: with one cheap haircut, I'd seemingly transformed from a radical to an undercover Fed.

For a while, I loved going to work. The routine and predictability were a welcome change from the improvised life I'd been living. I got a twenty-two-minute break every four hours. Given another half hour at lunchtime, I was soon chatting up all sorts of workers, getting a sense of mood and politics in this sprawling, noisy factory. Some of the older white guys hated commies with a passion and could smell me coming as soon as I opened my mouth about "the system." They were even more reactionary than Paul. Most of the black guys, especially the older ones, tended to be friendly. A few of the young "brothers" would only "tolerate" whites. But everything stayed cool because we received a similar paycheck and no one wanted to jeopardize that.

The work itself quickly became repetitive and mind dulling, but there was satisfaction in the good pay and full benefits, courtesy of the UAW. Class solidarity was helped by the fact that seniority was more important than race, at least until you got to upper management. We were the beneficiaries of decades of tough, persistent union organizing. You could resent the bosses and hate the job, but you could also buy a house and send your kids to college. It didn't take me long to appreciate that at one point in recent American history, the vanguard of the working class had been the union organizers. They didn't take over the government, but they brought countless big corporations to their knees. That was a whole lot more than what our movement had done. By 1971, the autoworkers had it pretty good. That was good news for the industrial working class and bad news for the prospects of a class revolution.

I worked the second shift, from 3:30 pm to 1:00 am. The drive took up to an hour each way: time to think and ponder. Gradually I began to accept that it was going to take more than racial inequality and a war six thousand miles away—even one that was killing their sons—to make my fellow workers fight to overthrow the system. And then, one rainy night as I made my way home, I was hit by the painful insight that my belief that a Marxist revolution that led to a classless, egalitarian society was all too similar to my old faith that Heaven awaited the true Christian believer. Both were fantasies conjured up by the faithful; there was no evidence that confessing my sins to a priest insured the way to heavenly bliss any more than a Marxist "proletarian dictatorship" was the way to reach a communist utopia. Hold on! I argued. Did that mean I had to make peace with our imperialistic, racist country? Another voice answered that at least ours wasn't a dictatorship. The system was grossly imperfect, but it had built in checks and balances on the extremes of human greed and ruthlessness. Besides, some inner-Buddhist weighed in, it's the all about the journey, not the destination.

None of those voices could alter the realization that I had traded in Jesus for Karl Marx, unconsciously replacing one belief system for another. Stunned, I had to admit that emotionally I had wanted something absolute to believe in and both my old religion and Marxism had delivered. Switching from Catholicism to Marxism hadn't disrupted my childhood religious indoctrination. Even though I thought I'd abandoned my belief in God, I had clung to my need for absolute answers. I remembered that boy who ran out of the church: once again I was rejecting the gift of faith. The grief I felt led me to understand that this time it was irrevocable.

As Stef's due date neared, we leaned inward, away from the war and the many lies of a compromised world. We decided against delivering the baby in a tub of warm water as some promoted, and instead, I became a birthing coach quite adept at the *hee-hee-hee* Lamaze breathing method. We arm-twisted a hospital in downtown LA to allow me stay in the delivery room. We brought in a portable tape player with East Indian shenai music as well as meditative art to help focus and soothe Stef. After eight hours she delivered a healthy, beautiful little girl. Awash in tears of joy and relief, I finally left the hospital as evening began and drove down the 10 Freeway into the sunset. My heart was bursting. Speeding along at sixty miles per hour in our VW van, I grabbed the tape deck and, right over that cassette of the shenai music, gave voice to all my wonder and awe. Pouring out what this new life meant to me, I expressed what must have been felt billions of times: as common a phenomenon as it was, the creation of a child seemed miraculous. It was the only miracle I could truly believe in: the miracle of life.

The next day, after we brought Jessica home, I played the tape for Stef as the baby suckled on her still gorgeous but wildly utilitarian breasts. Stef wept appreciatively at my heartfelt ramblings, then passed Jessica to me and disappeared for a much-needed nap. I anxiously held this delicate being and tried to burp her for the first time. Her rippling sonic release made me feel brilliant, and as I stared at her in my lap she emitted a similar sound from the other end of her tiny body. Unsure but undaunted, I embarked on my first diaper change. I could sense my child bringing me down to earth. I had wanted a kid, so I guess on some level I wanted to be grounded. Suddenly the biggest problem I faced was the damage that safety pins could do if Jessica squirmed at the wrong moment. I calmed myself down by imagining my mother doing the same for me many years before. I was part of a long line.

I barely slept that first night. I was exquisitely aware of Jessica beginning to master the art of living. In the early morning, when her whimpers roused me, I felt born again— not in the sense of taking up my old religion, but because I had given life to another. I realized that the gift of a child is the same gift we seek from religion: immortality. I had the sensation that through Jessica and however many other children I might have, and again through their children, I would never completely disappear even after I died and was forgotten. And, as far as securing a fair and just future, it had to begin with providing love and security for this little girl.

Sitting exhausted yet content before dawn on a June morning in 1971, rocking my firstborn back to sleep, I accepted that that was radical enough.

ACKNOWLEDGMENTS

This book began over two decades ago as a list of the events that made 1968 such an extraordinary year. It was meant as a way to explain what life was like "back in the day" to my curious and thoughtful daughters, Jessica Hicks and Tessa Hicks Peterson. It is my hope that my memoir will deepen their appreciation of the past and help them recognize and contend with the similarities to the present.

Several of those dear to me have passed away, including my parents, step-parents, my brother Jim Hicks, my sister Jean Miller and nephew Alex Miller, as well as Newsreel comrades: Jonathan Aurthur, Elinor Tideman Schiffrin Aurthur, and Christine Hansen. I've lost touched with many old friends, but I still enjoy the camaraderie and memory assistance of Michael Murphy, Peter Belsito, Judy Belsito, Bill Floyd and Ron Abrams. I deeply appreciate my readers, Deborah Cohen, Mark Waxman, Phoebe Larmore, and Stephanie Waxman, who gave critical feedback and encouragement.

I am grateful to several authors for their versions of the 60s. For his impressive, insightful research, I am indebted to Rick Perlstein's *Nixonland: The Rise of a President and the Fracturing of America* (Scribner, 2009). Along with many other examples of what made Nixon's presidency so dangerous is proof that in his effort to be elected in 1968, Nixon sabotaged the peace talks with North Vietnam. Perlstein also gives frightening details about Nixon's "mad man" tactic in 1969. For more information on that under-reported gamble on nuclear war, go to http://nsarchive.gwu.edu/nukevault/ebb517-Nixon-Kissinger-and-the-Madman-Strategy-during-Vietnam-War/.

A great deal of evidence confirming the FBI's murderous and undeclared war on the Black Panther Party is found in *Nixonland*. Also, *Black Against Empire: The History and Politics of the Black Panther Party* by Joshua Bloom and Waldo E. Martin, Jr. (Tantor Media, Inc., 2016) is very informative, as is: www.hartford-hwp.com/archives/45a/077.html. *Search for the New Land: History as Subjective Experience* (The Dial Press, 1969) by Julius Lester is another powerful reminder of those times. For her courageous memoir and intimate look into the Black Panther Party, especially in Los Angeles, I am thankful for Elaine Brown's *A Taste of Power: A Black Woman's Story* (Knopf Doubleday Publishing Group, 1993).

Martin Luther King Jr.'s article, "The Crisis in American Cities," can be found at http://noirg.org/articles/dr-martin-luther-kings-forgotten-writings/.

Krishnamurti's quote is from *Freedom from the Known*, Chapter 15, (Harper One, 2009)

The complete interview about shooting longhairs is in *Kent State: What Happened and Why* by James Michener, page 454, (Random House, 1971)

David James, Professor of Cinema at the University of Southern California, explored Los Angeles Newsreel in depth in his article, *An Impossible Cinema*, Film International #2 (2003:2) and in his book, *The Most Typical Avant-Garde: History and Geography of Minor Cinemas in Los Angeles* (University of California Press, 2006). I deeply appreciate his interest and support.

Further details about Los Angeles Newsreel are available from interviews of Dennis Hicks, Stephanie Waxman, and Peter Belsito conducted by Jane Collings for the Center for Oral History Research, University of California, Los Angeles. (2005)

A more general history of Newsreel can be found in *Newsreel: Film and Revolution* (Master's thesis, University of California, Los

Angeles, 1972) by Bill Nichols, and in his book, *Newsreel: Documentary Filmmaking on the American Left* (New York: Arno, 1980).

Repression, the twelve-minute rough cut of Los Angeles Newsreel's portrayal of the Los Angeles Black Panther Party and the struggle for an international working-class revolution, was recovered in 1997. You can see it at http://uschefnerarchive.com/ project/dennis-hicks- collection/ along with some of the original footage and outtakes from that project. The film is included in the DVD collection: *What We Want, What We Believe*, The Black Panther Party Library, AK Press, 2006.

My work in documentary film, public television and educational media from 1975-1983 has been collected at the University of Southern California's SCA Hugh M. Hefner Moving Image Archive: http://uschefnerarchive.com/ project/dennis-hicks- collection/. Many thanks to Dino Everett, Archivist, for his thoughtful labors.

POST SCRIPT

In 1974, three years after this memoir ends, I left General Motors to teach elementary school. During the next ten years I produced a wide range of media on the social and educational benefits of school desegregation and racial integration. In the late-80's, I began a psychotherapy practice from which I retired in 2012. I published a novel, *Camera Obscura*, in 2007. I am married to author Stephanie Waxman and we have two daughters and five grandchildren. For more, please visit *http://www.dennishicks.net*.

Made in the USA
San Bernardino, CA
11 January 2018